1 DIALOGUE INTRODUCTION

"Architects have to take risks again, have to be specialists, have to be authorities, and have to take the Metropolis as their domain for technological production and invention. The city will be silent, noiseless, and clean, and the new domain for production and live/life; the domain for slowness; the domain for diversity. New discoveries, new risks, new expeditions are now taking researchers to "outer space," without comfort. Mars, Pluto, and Jupiter will challenge us, give us new content, and give us new opportunities to overcome, the Modern."

—Wiel Arets, "A Wonderful World," *MCHAP: The Americas 1* (New York/Chicago: Actar/IITAC, 2016).

Every intervention in and on the Skin of the Earth, should be questioned, as should its relevance; the discovery of unknown life in the oceans and the impact of the deep interior of the globe, will have profound impacts on the evolution of human life. Nowadays, we are exploring outer space and discovering, for example, that life on Mars has had an impact, on life on Earth. We are starting to understand that every fingerprint will change the subtle ecological and physical equilibrium that exists within the cosmos. Whether we consider the research done by Alexander von Humboldt, regarding different ecosystems, or "progressive research," with all the knowledge that we can be confronted with, every day; we will read scientific discoveries as significant, and relevant for the future of human life. The impact we as a species will have on the total universe is, perhaps, not even worth considering—although many believe differently. Architecture and urbanism are violent acts of cutting into the Skin of the Earth, which change existing urban or natural landscapes, and create orientation and disorientation. I strongly believe that the moment architects strategize about architecture or urbanism, as a concept or idea, I would call it an act of interiority; that is, the essence of architecture. Architec-

ture is a part of our collective effort, and collaboration is needed for it; that's why discourse about the impact it has had or will have on our physical landscape, is the main factor for our academic approach. We defined this approach as: NOWNESS. Sometimes we can start seemingly fresh, by building new cities and new metropolises on seemingly untouched sites, though we must also ask ourselves whether what we now know, is relevant for a new beginning. Having a discourse, having a dialogue, or having a debate are different words used to express different thoughts, and are to be used in different contexts; but what they have in common is that they ask for time to think, to re-think. The architectural dialogue has given the possibility to young architects, to formulate their reading and structure their arguments about how to deal with our reality, consciously and unconsciously, and how to construct a language one can work with. The platform for this constructed dialogue, and for positioning themselves, and for testing their arguments, has been fruitful to all. The College of Architecture's "Dean's Dialogues" events have been structured around the "Rethinking Metropolis" discourse, and were prepared by students—who we prefer to call young architects—and faculty. Authorities in different disciplines were invited to present their vision on a topic regarding the city that they have been concentrating on, and have previously published about. Students and faculty researched these topics and studied the work by our guests, and initiated ongoing written and vocal conversations—dialogues. While at S. R. Crown Hall, our guests were confronted with several questions prepared by our students and faculty, all structured around a challenging viewpoint. Since the dialogues were meant to be beneficial to all, they are only loosely structured, since the flow of intense conversations gave everyone the chance to be engaged and develop their own ideas. Being confronted with arguments, architects, designers, and artists were invited to present their own visions. They were challenged to focus on relevant issues that they wished to put forward. They were challenged by the debates during studio critiques, but also while engaged with an audience, who responded to their lectures. The process of transformation and learning, of re-formulating, because of these intense and recorded dialogues, had an immediate impact on the public lectures, which were given at night, on the same day, and all of which were digitally streamed. Private dialogues and public debates in S. R. Crown Hall should be articulated in an exchange with lecturers, who present attitudes of resistance by confronting their audiences, and by virtue of streaming their thoughts out into the world. Dealing with chaos, understanding that conflict is part of the process, and that the development of a vision does not happen in isolation, but by confronting and developing ideas with others–this is central to the academic institution we believe in. To bring such antagonists into the arena of S. R. Crown Hall–the largest classroom in the world–and have a dialogue about the complex mechanisms of our local and global enterprises, must be considered as breaking the limits of what is possible. Developing a new or renewed vision for the metropolis, with the forces and fields of operation and participation, questions the discipline of architecture, the domain that it works within, the process of making, the introduction of the digital and the virtual domains, and of course, the expectations of the society and community in which we operate. How will the human, body and mind, anticipate and develop within this ultimately amazing venture; at a time in which the individual is confronted with new domains and renewed expectations and in which inside and outside asks for continual redefinition.

Wiel Arets, Chicago, May 1, 2017

KAZUYO SEJIMA
WILLIAM BAKER
WIEL ARETS
JUNYA ISHIGAMI
STEFANO BOERI
PETER EISENMAN
RAFAEL VIÑOLY
BEN VAN BERKEL
PEZO VON ELLRICHSHAUSEN
PHYLLIS LAMBERT
RIKEN YAMAMOTO
HERMAN HERTZBERGER
ERWIN OLAF
DAVID ADJAYE
ARMAND MEVIS
DOMINIQUE PERRAULT
STAN ALLEN
BERNARD KHOURY

7   OPENNESS
KAZUYO SEJIMA

> You co-founded SANAA even as you maintained your individual practice, Kazuyo Sejima & Associates. What role does each practice play in guiding your architecture?

Sejima: From the beginning, we thought that it is important that sometimes we are able to collaborate and sometimes we are independent and separate. To this day, our work continues to be very different. We may seem similar, next to other architects, but for us there are big differences in our work. We are collaborating more often, however, because we get projects based on what we have already done, making it hard to choose between working separately or together. So I cannot say that the role of each is clear, because while we work on a lot of SANAA projects together, we also have our separate projects, making us overlap and collaborate often, blurring the distinctions.

> Your drawings are simple, almost child-like; what does this approach to representation do for you?

Sejima: It's because we don't know how to draw! [Laughs]. Basically, I like making the building not in opposition to the body, but as a continuation of it. When it is easy [makes hand gesture, as if sketching], or more smoothly connected by the motion of the hand, it continues into the weight of the building, and into the distance between things. One aspect is the aesthetics of it, but the other is the continuity of the body.

SANAA, GRACE FARMS, NEW CANAAN,
CONNECTICUT, 2015.

Speaking of continuity, in many of your buildings, you use glass as partitions. What is the role of transparency in your work?

Sejima: Recently, it has become less about transparency. While glass is important visually, for me it is also about the role it can have to make diversity possible. Mies [van der Rohe]'s buildings are very transparent, for example here in S. R. Crown Hall, where studios, offices, and conference spaces can happen together. When I hear a noise from other activities in here, it does not disturb me, but if it was in a different type of building, even the smallest noise could be very uncomfortable. The atmosphere in here allows people to be together while doing different things. The glass makes an atmosphere of different social interactions possible.

Do you consider the use of glass to be a social act?

Sejima: Somehow yes, but it is about the openness also. In different shapes and designs, glass sometimes becomes very hard and divides things up quite severely. It is also very difficult to use—the thickness and the materiality make it very sensitive. I have realized that even people who do not study architecture can feel with their bodies when glass is very thick and divisive, as opposed to when it is soft and continuous. People can feel these things, so the size and proportion, the detailing, and the composition are all important.

Does the softening and distortion of lines and edges through transparencies relate to your conception of contemporary public space?

Sejima: One of my interests, from the very beginning, is in finding the relation between inside and outside. In every project, I have tried to achieve that in different ways by relating it to the program. In the Glass Pavilion at the

Toledo Museum of Art [2006], every program is made up of curved glass partitions. People can see through these spaces, but at the same time the curved glass is very reflective, so you always see the real and the reflected scenery together as one. But it is not just about the visual effect of the curved glass, it is also about how it changes social relationships as you move through the space.

> Your work appears to be extremely domestic—as if you are at home—perhaps because it is always related to the body. Even when the buildings become bigger, you still keep the human scale and domestic feeling, which is very unique. Is this something you consciously think about?

Sejima: The possibilities of different scales vary quite a lot. I don't want to start with the domestic and scale up to big architecture. However, at the same time, the notion of the domestic itself is not necessarily a man-made one. I don't know the precise meaning of "domestic," but it feels natural, not made.

> Domestic doesn't mean small. It is the feeling of being at home, and even when you do big buildings, people feel at home.

Sejima: People can always find their own private feeling, even when they are in a big building. I want to make spaces that people can touch and not feel rejected by. Everyone can then start to find ways to connect and make relationships to the spaces in their own ways. At the same time, I want to make small objects or houses that keep the abstract distance of strength and comfort.

> You emphasize non-hierarchy through the diffusion of spaces and free circulation in your buildings. Why is this important to you?

Sejima: This has been important for me since the beginning. Light has to come from everywhere in order to avoid hierarchy. I wanted to make spaces that people can develop reactions to, and imagine new ways of using by themselves, which is why we make so many possibilities for circulation and entry. Of course, we can also make a very beautiful private house that one person inhabits as a king or queen, but a building for 300 people is more interesting. Transparency allows diversity and openness, and it is important to make space in which different people can spend time together comfortably, and where they can imagine and respect differences.

> Contemporary Japanese architects—at least from an outsider's point-of-view—share similar aesthetics and ideologies. Why do you think that is?

Sejima: Compared to European architecture, it may seem similar, but for me it is so different. In Europe, space is made by the thickness of a wall, whereas historically, in Japan, it's always been much thinner. Dean [Wiel] Arets invited me to the Berlage Institute a long time ago, and I tried to explain openness, but nobody understood it. So I slowly realized that in the European context, openness just means open, but in Japan there is a deeper and more nuanced discussion of open and closed. It was quite a local Japanese term that maybe has gotten more relatable in the past twenty years. When we Japanese talk about openness, even if it is quite different between us, it appears similar to the non-Japanese.

> How do you define the word openness?

Sejima: Openness is not just about physicality. It is more about continuity, sharing, and the relationship between people.

KAZUYO SEJIMA AT GRACE FARMS, NEW CANAAN,
CONNECTICUT, JUNE 2016.

You simplify and reduce elements in your architecture, can you explain why?

Sejima: I think we have changed since our early projects; it might still look simple but it has become more complicated. After the EPFL Learning Centre [2010] project, we have actively tried to bring the smaller scale in, whereas before, when we were trying to find the relationship between inside and outside, the concept of the outside was more abstract. For example, with the IIT campus, we summarized the environment and abstracted the campus, but now we see the campus as more diverse and specific, with the chapel and different facades. We approach the outside not as an abstract generic entity, but as smaller-scale specificities; it is a different way to do it, although maybe still simple.

How do you approach the relationship of the building to its site?

Sejima: During EPFL, I realized that the building is difficult to connect to its surroundings, even though the shape is organic and made of glass. If the structure is one system, the building has a strong character and appears to be unified. I used to rely on the continuity given by the horizontal movement of the roof and floor through bracing and thick supporting walls, but with independent structures, each space can stand on its own but be connected, so I tried to bring in more curves. Before, I wanted to make buildings that are integrated into the landscape, but now I think the buildings themselves should be a part of the landscape. It is not about the connection between building and landscape anymore but, hopefully now the building forgets that it is a building and becomes part of the environment.

Your architecture is usually highly technological and engineered. How much control do you have over the final form as the architect and not the engineer?

Sejima: There is more information to consider today than ever before, making more collaboration necessary. I learn from the suggestions of others, but I also try to maybe not control, but guide things. In EPFL, the engineers made many simulations, and it was the structure, sound, energy, and climate that determined the final plan. The courtyards started as childish sketches, but when we had to make the molds for the curved glass it became a potato curve made up of nine or ten straight lines, which completely changed the shapes of the courtyards. The positions of the courtyard were adjusted because the structural engineers had to find ways to reduce the weight of the structure. The sound engineer also contributed to the final plan with their sound partitions. This process was guided by us, but we also could not have made the plan without the engineering suggestions.

In Japan, there is a strong respect accorded to legacies. What ideas from the past have you been interested in?

Sejima: Japanese architecture existed naturally, so when I was young, I didn't take it very seriously. The concept of architecture in Japan started with the Modern movement, whereas before, we didn't think of it as architecture but more as structure. I have realized over time that there are many things to learn from vernacular Japanese architecture, such as the importance of how to make and construct; proportion, too. The connection between different parts is not hidden in Japanese wood construction, rather, it is very clear how the force is carried to the ground.

How do you see the future of the discipline?

Sejima: We have talked about history, but I'm very happy

that now we are at a point where all of us architects think about the future. Continuously, but especially now, everyone tries to think about and find new positions for where architecture should stand. In that sense, I'm very happy to be here, and to think again.

WILLIAM BAKER

As a structural engineer that has worked in tandem with architects for most of your career, could you comment on the specific rewards and challenges that relationship entails?

Baker: My experience with architects has mostly been at Skidmore, Owings & Merrill LLP (SOM), which is an integrated practice: engineers of various types (structural, mechanical, electrical, and sustainable) work with architects, as well as urban planners, interior designers, and graphic designers, to cite just a few disciplines. This was the primary context for my professional development. It's a free and open environment. We try to begin each project with everybody at the table, and conduct meetings in a very open manner throughout. Input is welcomed on a broad range of topics, irrespective of your field. I might find myself talking about landscaping, for example. SOM is a kind of self-selecting society made up of architects who like working with engineers, and engineers who like working with architects. It is very rewarding, in my opinion, although there are downsides as well. Design issues are worked over thoroughly, with a great deal of communication, but the back-and-forth can become laborious. We have these so-called kindergarten tables around our office to facilitate discussion. They were explicitly set up for up to eight people to use. These impromptu conversations between disciplines are the reason we get better designs.

From a structural engineering perspective, is your main agenda the structural engineering of a project, or have you instilled architectural values in your design methodology?

Baker: I am mindful of architectural values as they express the space and tell the stories that are crucial to the reception of the overall design. Structural design values are relevant insofar as they communicate how the building works, how the technology of that building is expressed, and, like architecture, tell the narrative of the building structure. Both are crucial if the building is to work. The perfect structure isn't often the best building, just as the perfect exterior or perfect interior or perfect mechanical system alone isn't often the best building. It's more than simply holding the line on some concept or idea. The important principles to follow when setting your agenda are knowing what's relevant to what you're doing, as well as when and where each discipline can be implemented to make the building better. Knowing these things establishes an understanding of collaboration and compromise. Sometimes you have to challenge your collaborators on their criteria; at other times they might challenge you. Do not underestimate another profession's ability to solve problems. Though you may have to compromise on your end alone for the good of the project, more often than not, it will be a collaborative process. To sum up, our abilities as structural engineers are not defined by simply finding a solution.

Don't these collaborative relationships vary across project scales and types? Supertall buildings, for example, are intensely concentrated on engineering. What role does the architect play in these changed circumstances?

Baker: Everything plays an important role in supertall buildings, or any large building, not just engineering. The structure is very dominant, and we may have a million solutions, but each solution will have a million different architectural implications. So what we often do is a menu of solutions—that is to say, a list of options to ascertain the implications of all the proposed systems. With each structural solution, questions are asked regarding implications for the architectural representation, and with each architecture solution, questions are asked about the structural implications. The menu allows us to discover the right questions and answers for each supertall building; if the structure is too complicated, too expensive, or too difficult to build, it probably won't get built due to economies of scale. So the architect remains essential— the whole team in fact. Often an idea is filtered through everyone else's ideas and the original idea will morph into something no one had conceived to start with. I can say that I have never come away from a meeting with the same idea as when I entered the meeting. Yes, there are certain principles everyone is made aware of with regards to what is important or not, but the basis of every building begins with the whole team, regardless of scale.

> Do you believe we will be capable of realizing something similar to Frank Lloyd Wright's mile high tower in the near future? For example, you have noted that the buttressed core system you developed for the 828-meter tall Burj Khalifa could easily extend to a mile, but current technology would still restrict the height.

Baker: There is a point at which I would move away from the buttress core system—there are probably better systems for a mile high tower. One of the most important things to consider at such a height is scale. In Myron Goldsmith's graduate thesis, which was undertaken for Hilberseimer and Mies at IIT in 1953, there is an essay outlining these issues. It includes a sketch by Galileo of two bones from different creatures: a big bulky bone and a slender bone. Both bones have the same length, but completely different proportions. One can understand that a change in size manifests itself as a change of scale, and can require an entirely different creature or a different species to solve the problem. Goldsmith demonstrated this with a chart of several bridges with different spans, whereby each span corresponded to a different creature. Nature has provided structural solutions through the process of evolution, but humans can actually bypass evolution and proceed straight to creation. We can create a whole new species. The cable-stayed bridge is not even mentioned in Goldsmith's catalogue of bridge types. It became prominent only when the Germans used it widely after World War II, and it became a new species, or type, of bridge. The one thing we can do as designers is to invent new species. That's what the buttressed core is: it's a new species that lives at a certain range. Its efficiencies do not manifest above or below a certain height, giving it a certain range of efficient use. Now, going back to the issues of super-tall buildings, one of the issues that arises regardless of structure is air pressure. At one mile there is significant pressure—ears begin to pop, or they don't if people have head colds. Humans need time to adjust to a change in elevation and this has a large effect on the elevator speeds that can be permitted. Even the first "skyscraper" here in Chicago, the Home Insurance Building, had two major issues: structure and vertical transportation. The same issues still occur at a mile. The challenge given to us by the market is to maximize the usable floor area on a plot that is still desirable and comfortable.

> In one of your lectures, you appear to be very critical of what you call "willful excess." Could you elaborate on your understanding of the term, and how it relates to supertall buildings?

Baker: Willful excess may be described as that which is not of substantive importance to the architecture. I believe in substantive architecture, which—from the perspective of my profession—is related to the building being recognizable for what it actually is, whether that's function or technology. A building should not relate to the ego of the designer, or to the willfulness of the designer to make something. I am fairly critical of willfulness, particularly when it is wasteful of resources and adds a giant carbon footprint. I freely admit, however, that the ethics of the supertall building are not totally clear either. At a certain height, they're very economical due to their density. They are good for the culture of cities, because they get people closer together. It is clear the world requires inspirational projects and special buildings of difference. The example I like to use is the Eiffel Tower, which is essentially a very expensive way to build a restaurant. But Paris would be diminished—and so would France, or Europe, or the world—without the Eiffel Tower. From an aesthetic perspective, the Eiffel Tower is a clear expression of its technology, so I don't see it as willful. Yet, it was certainly a major act of ego to create such an edifice. The Burj Khalifa's success is beyond what we could have predicted; it has been a hugely significant object for Dubai, for the UAE, and for our client for that matter. It hosts an incredible light show on New Year's Eve. It has been a great attractor for people, who want to live or be around it. Our client actually made most of their money from selling the buildings around it!

> From an architectural perspective, the big difference between steel and concrete is that concrete has mass, or an accumulation we might say. So it has a lot of advantages for a designer that steel does not. Would you agree?

Baker: I'm a minimalist, so I prefer it when I can make steel members smaller and more delicate. Several years ago, I was working on a project at the Roden Crater with

WILLIAM BAKER, POSTER OF "THE ENGINEERING OF ARCHITECTURE" EXHIBITION, MUNICH, GERMANY, JANUARY–MARCH, 2016.

the artist James Turrell. He and I were making a pitch to a group of potential donors for a new part of the crater called "The Fumeral." Our argument was that we could make it buildable by infusing some hierarchy, order, and clarity into the project. I said that what we brought to the table was Miesian simplicity. Suddenly, James corrects me and says, "No, no, Quaker simplicity," because James was raised as a Quaker. So I started attending Quaker services in order to understand what he meant, and discover how simplicity could relate to both Quakers and Mies. From what I understood of Quakers, they are raised to value simplicity in speech, dress, and food; one of their key phrases is to "step into the light." James transferred these ethical values into his art. Suddenly, when viewing his work with its vision of simplicity and light, you realize his constructions are not even physical. Our eyes construct from the light. He led me to start thinking about my ethical position in regards to my aesthetic position. I made a list of things that I value, and soon realized my preferences for simplicity over complexity was related to the Calvinist way I was raised. There are moral overtones to them, such as one shouldn't be overly wasteful. I stress simplicity because I value hierarchy, harmony, and elegance, which all foster, "appropriateness." This also relates to one of the things I truly hate, which is applied structures, where structure is used as decoration.

> SOM's latest research project proposes a solution to tall timber construction with the use of a concrete-jointed timber frame. What are your thoughts on this proposal?

Baker: We carried out some very interesting studies on the appropriate use of timber and how to optimize it. Assume a situation where one has to construct five buildings, and there is a limited amount of wood available. Under normal circumstances, one building would be made entirely from timber, and the other four would be constructed in concrete or steel. This is an inefficient use of materials, because each material hasn't been used where it is most valuable. Our research aimed to find out where the timber is most efficiently used, in order to spread the timber across the five buildings and reduce the carbon footprint of concrete and steel. We benchmarked the proposal against the Chestnut-Dewitt building by Myron Goldsmith and Fazlur Khan, which is their most efficient concrete high-rise project. That building used approximately one cubic foot of concrete per square-foot of floor plate (taking into account all the concrete in the building, slabs, walls, spandrel beams, and columns). Of that cubic foot, eight inches is accounted for by the slabs, and four inches is accounted by the rest. From this simple calculation, it became obvious that we could save the most concrete in the slabs. Another excellent example of efficient material use is the Brooklyn Bridge. The bridge is a long span, lightweight structure comprised of steel cables that supports the deck, and masonry portions that resist the compression loads. The key idea is to put the material where it is the most useful. I also believe that a building should be able to achieve more than one usage, or one layout, if it is to survive. With our composite timber-and-concrete system, we found that we can achieve longer spans with fewer vertical obstructions. This allows a building, such as an apartment building, to take on several lives, for example, if an occupant wants to expand their apartment without obstruction from several load-bearing walls. Most timber proposals nowadays are based on nineteenth century technology that necessitate lots of columns and walls—which just creates rabbit warrens that you can't change. With normal leases in the United States being around ten years, the spaces we create must be able to accommodate changes, for example, from a law office, to a tech office, to an open office. Thus, longer spans, fewer columns, and fewer obstructions are an implicit goal, so that a building can have a longer shelf life.

What are the benefits and the perils of using wood as a high-rise building material?

Baker: The biggest drawbacks of wood are fireproofing and dimensional stability, that is, the variation in length. It is crucial to think about the dimensional stability of wood over the seasons and its implications for tall buildings. And of course, fireproofing must be taken care of above all else. After that, the main benefit of using wood is to minimize our carbon footprint. As tall building people, we have looked at the problem of timber high-rises from the perspective of structural systems, whereas the wood people start with their knowledge of the material itself. Probably neither of us has hit on the right solution yet, but I'm sure we'll end up somewhere closer to each other in the end.

What has your experience been with long-span structures, and what are its inherent potentials and limitations?

Baker: I like long-span structures a lot. They don't receive as much attention as high-rises, but there is a lot of room for creativity in a long-span. The boundary conditions are much more complex compared to tall buildings, and the design process is actually a search for constraints. Whereas a cantilevered tall building has only one path to carry the load down, a long span has multiple paths, which leads to many more questions about the spans and their placement. The process consists of finding a set of rules that strategically constrain the design. In fact, we are undertaking research at this very moment on developing new design methodologies for long-span structures. Our research has taken us into shells and grid shells, which are producing amazing results while remaining quite accessible to us. They don't require a PhD in differential equations and differential geometry.

Given your interest in reducing the amount of materials and embodied energy in sustainable tall buildings, how do you tackle the problem?

Baker: Geometry—the single most important parameter in structure is geometry. It is where architecture and structure meet: the former describes a space in geometric terms, just as the latter involves expressing a building geometrically. However, once a geometry is chosen, it is locked in; a limit has been placed on the efficiency of the structure. The limitations of that geometry can be huge. So our number one priority for reducing materials is determining the right geometry and the right system. I often use the very simple example of a building where one solution uses 60 percent more material than the other, yet visually the two solutions appear to be similar. 60 percent more! Talk about carbon footprint. With all the varieties of complex geometry being discovered today, we need to consider how to find and naturalize these geometries. Many of our solutions look very organic, almost like biomimicry. I'm not a fan of biomimicry in an aesthetic sense, where the objective is to make a building look like a plant. Rather, I'm interested in the D'Arcy Thompson approach—people forget he was as much a mathematician and physicist as he was a biologist—he studied organisms through the lens of engineering mechanics, to understand the real physics of their materials, surface tension, and so on. Thompson believed that the reason the creatures he studied look like they do is because they are a solution to a physics problem. Similarly, I aim to describe the problem a building has in terms of the physics of the problem, and the loads it is trying to transmit. Some of the tools we use to solve these problems may give us very organic-looking solutions, but they're not directly adapted from a plant, or anything like that.

> Which material would you say has the most potential to push the boundaries of architectural and engineering production?

Baker: That's a loaded question. I try not to have favorites. When I start designing, I'm completely agnostic about the material, whether it's steel, glass, timber, concrete, or something else. I love steel, from a mathematics perspective. Glass is amazing stuff—it weighs as much as granite, but has the stiffness of aluminum, and is transparent. Certainly, timber's going to be the thing for the next decade or two. I think we'll really figure out how to use timber in a modern way, which is a good thing because it is much better to store carbon in buildings that last a long time. Bamboo is stronger than wood, but the glue used to laminate the small pieces of bamboo together is definitely not sustainable. Concrete has tremendous potential, because the chemistry can be altered to completely change its qualities. The concrete today is so different from what was used for sidewalks that it probably deserves a different name; it's become a very strong and stiff material, that's getting stiffer and stiffer with a higher and higher modulus of elasticity. For the Burj Khalifa concrete, the modulus was extremely high.

> The ideas in architecture tend to be based on static objects, as opposed to the car and aerospace industries where movement is critical. The Zeppelins, for example, were a transitory housing object. Could you talk a little bit about bringing those criteria into architecture?

Baker: I have a book, *Housing the Airship* [ed. Christopher Dean, Architectural Association, 1989], with photographs of the inside of a Zeppelin during construction. The im-

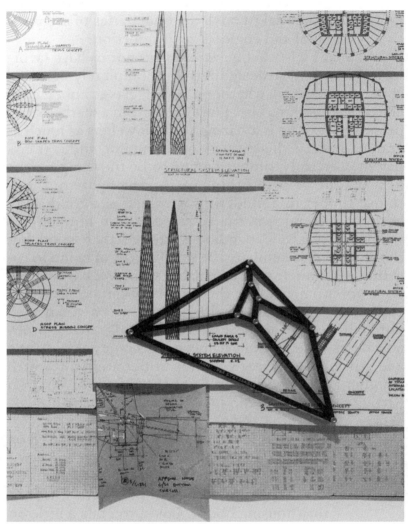

WILLIAM BAKER, "THE ENGINEERING OF
ARCHITECTURE" EXHIBITION, MUNICH,
GERMANY, JANUARY–MARCH, 2016. THE EXHIBIT
FEATURED MORE THAN TWENTY ICONIC SOM
SKYSCRAPERS WITH UNIQUE STRUCTURAL
ENGINGEERING SOLUTIONS.

ages are unbelievably beautiful. It was simply a series of bicycle wheels, all beautifully aligned, where the outside hoops are stressed to the ring in the center through the tension cables. The engineers physically weighed every piece before installation to compare the estimated weight and the actual weight to ensure the Zeppelin would actually take off. Again, all of this relates to geometry, and learning to ask meaningful questions about it. About seven years ago, we contacted an engineer in Stuttgart, Ekkehard Ramm, who instigated studies in form finding and new geometries. So we called up the professor and asked if we could use his software. He said no, but he did inform us that he had sold a version of it to Altair in Michigan. Altair's software was used to design the window and wings on an Airbus. So eventually we got them to come see us, and tried to explain why we wanted to talk to them about new geometries. Since then, we've been getting a lot of other software that allows us to model very sophisticated things, and collaborate with a lot of highly theoretical academics in various civil engineering departments, all of whom are trying to figure out what a natural structure is, and then how we can interpret that. These exercises create knowledge that the designer then figures out how to apply, whether it's to static or mobile architectures.

> Maintaining the building climate is becoming a larger challenge with the increasing size, or mass, of tall buildings. What are your thoughts on such challenges?

Baker: In my home, I have wood flooring with radiant heat, and it works very well—even though the wood has low thermal mass. So I'm curious as to how many different ways there are to do it. We now know that water is a very efficient way of transmitting energy, much more than blowing air around. There is a tremendous amount of energy expended on fans in tall buildings, so to the extent that water can be used as a medium to move energy, there is a great opportunity for efficiency in the systems for the climate of a building. Don't get me wrong: the high thermal mass of a concrete building floor goes a long way towards creating pleasant spaces. However, it is still all about how to manipulate the energy transfer, whether it's through your hands and feet, or through your head.

> Given your previous comments on the changing nature of concrete, especially its composition, what would you say is the future of concrete, including ferroconcrete?

Baker: 3D printing of concrete is opening up the field tremendously. I recently spoke to someone who was researching bones. Now, bones are not solid—they have several tiny voids that facilitate blood flow as well as structural efficiency. Thus, the nature of bone construction is also related to mechanical circulation. I can see high-strength concrete having a similar impact on structure, whereby voids are created in the structure where the strength isn't needed to facilitate another function. It could even be multiple uses of different kinds of concrete in one system. Such variation in concrete's material composition could even lead to a form of three-dimensional complex laminate, or composite panel, where the panel is produced three-dimensionally, rather than just a buildup of layers. Yet, I would also warn against complete optimization. There's a poem by Oliver Wendell Holmes called "The One-Hoss Shay" about Calvinism that applies: there is a preacher whose buggy was as pure as his religion, in which everything fit together perfectly. Yet when the buggy wore down, it disintegrated completely. The wheels fell off, the carpet tore, and everything else completely disintegrated. The point I want to make is that when everything is optimized at the limit at the same time, everything can fail in a fairly dramatic way, too.

In the course of your career, you have simultaneously engaged in writing, building, and teaching. Which do you believe has had the largest impact on the discipline of architecture?

Arets: Each has its own impact on architecture. Writing about your discipline opens your mind. There are books, or even short quotes by architects, that have had an incredible impact. The earliest books by Vitruvius or Palladio still have a strong resonance in the discipline. When you build, it's a process that leads to an extremely clear end result; you can make conceptual statements while being clear about what your position is. It's the same difference as cinema and art, or literature. With building, the architect that deals with theory as well as many other components is very successful. Academia provides very different criteria for behaviors, thoughts, and words. They are three parallel tracks, which merge; they are equally important. Some architects only deal with one: they build. Some architects are theoreticians who only write. You can't say that one has a bigger impact than the others.

In the United States, architects are typically expected to design buildings while in Europe, designing "from the spoon to the city" is a common idea. How have architects in Europe managed to maintain a broader spectrum of work, whereas architectural work has narrowed to specializations in the United States?

Arets: I think there are certain periods in history that have that momentum. The furniture designs by Charles Eames and other architects are still extremely important—in that moment, American architects designed everything. It was the same with Frank Lloyd Wright, and Mies van der Rohe when he was in America. There are many other examples where American architects designed many of their building interiors. It's not always a typical European thing, I think. And now it transcends borders. Let's say I am working with Alessi, where Alberto Alessi has asked architects around the world to design for him; the work may be produced in Europe, but it's distributed all over. That's an example of the global production and distribution of design that is common today.

> Certainly, Eames and Wright designed much of their buildings—interior, exterior, furniture, and overall—but why is it so much rarer, recently?

Arets: It may have to do with all the disciplines and sub-disciplines working together in the United States. First you have the urban planner, then the building architect, and maybe the program architect, or the architect who deals with the interior. You see more and more of these projects that are being divided up and handed off as if they are different jobs. Personally, I like to do buildings from A to Z. That's also what I negotiate with our clients. And even when we work with other designers, we discuss the team we are going to work with and build it together. We have always done urban design, and, of course buildings, but we also made products like the Hot.It water cooker and the Il Bagno dOt complete bathroom set; it consists of everything from a bathtub to soap dishes. One of our most recent projects is cutlery, which we also designed for Alessi. So that whole range—from cutlery to urban design; it interests me. But I don't think it's a typical European thing; it's happened in America and it's still happening as well.

To build on your reference to forming a team, in your introduction to the new curriculum at IIT, you emphasized expanding the role of architects and entering into dialogue with multiple disciplines. What do you believe are the key qualities that young architects must acquire today for future success?

Arets: When you are part of a team, you have to understand the total concept for the project that you are working on. You also have to understand what the other team members are dealing with—each team member always has responsibility for other team members. You can't say, "Oh, I'll just do this while the others are doing that." Yes, you make a specific contribution, but you must have the full perspective. I strongly believe that when you talk about IIT, its curriculum comes from the faculty, and all of the members of the faculty have to understand what the bigger idea of the school is. "Rethinking Metropolis" is not simply a title. Let's acknowledge that the metropolis has a history and a lot to offer, but we also have to move forward and recognize that in a moment when there are so many disciplines involved in every decision, it is impossible to think that you can do things by yourself. You have to operate in a team and you have to be strategic. In the case of the school, the important questions revolve around what you can achieve, and how you can work with other faculty, or even other colleges at IIT. What can they offer us, but also, what we can offer them? What do other institutions in the city have to offer and how can we be in exchange with them? We want our students to understand from their first day at this school that we have a kind of blueprint ready for them: which trajectories, how each project is dealing with a certain idea, and the knowledge that it's all part of a bigger process that doesn't end with the Director of Theory and History, or the person who is dealing with structural engineering.

WIEL ARETS ARCHITECTS, UTRECHT UNIVERSITY
LIBRARY, UTRECHT, THE NETHERLANDS, 2004.

Everyone, including the students, should instantly know that they are part of a team and they should understand the goal of the team that they are working with.

> Just this year, Stan Allen, Ben van Berkel, Winy Maas, Tham & Videgård (and even yourself a couple of years ago) have mentioned the slowness of architecture in lectures. Is this something that we are actively resisting?

Arets: Paul Virilio once said that we move physically at a faster and faster rate with the invention of new technology. We transitioned from walking, to riding animals, to driving cars, and now launching rockets, and are starting to understand how we can use gravity and anti-gravity to bring us in orbit. All of that deals with the capacity to move in a physical way. But our perception has shifted too: digital technology has helped us to understand and communicate with each other differently, which adds to our concept of speed in the modern world. Similarly, not only is the architectural process slow, it is slow in different ways. Over the last two millennia, architecture has changed, but it has not changed as much as people believe it has. Every generation believes everything has radically changed. That's just not the case. The second thing to note is that slowness also has to do with the process of building, which always takes a couple of years. In these couple of years you have to make thousands of decisions, in a team of people who operate at a slightly different speed from each other, or at a slightly different momentum. The team may not even have the exact same end result, or the same knowledge in mind. Slowness in this case has to do with the production of the project, aside from the production of ideas. Third, technological developments can be extremely quick and revolutionary. But buildings in the metropolitan condition change much more slowly. We can choose certain materials to build with, like steel, brick, concrete, aluminum, or glass, and we can test these materials within their structural possibilities over time. Glass, concrete, or steel with new technologies are being used, and have different conditions than maybe ten or fifteen years ago, but people moving through these buildings may not see that incremental change. Finally, slowness may also have to do with the people that make use of the building, if they contemplate, rather than move through it hurriedly in a distracted way. Slowness is part of the process for how to perceive a building—time slows down. So perhaps architecture can play a useful part in the cultural counter-reaction that has been brewing in response to our frenetic pace of life. At the same time that people are flying in airplanes or rockets at incredible speeds, they are also developing the new Zeppelin, where you can get from America to Asia in forty days. That development is really interesting to see. People have started to think, is it possible to be extremely slow, and bring ourselves to a very different condition?

> Rem Koolhaas once remarked that an architect has not been on the cover of "Time Magazine" in decades. Do architects still have the potential to impact society like inventors and entrepreneurs or those from other occupations?

Arets: We live in a world where the media highlights certain issues that people want to read about. That builds momentum. There is always momentum behind someone famous who thinks up something, and the whole world concentrates on that for a few years. It's momentum that has impact on the way the world changes. Meanwhile, we ignore the documentary that is telling us that we are using our resources in a way that will fundamentally shift how the world will be operating, in just a couple of years. So in the second instance, new technologies eventually have an impact. New technologies exist because of entrepreneurs that want to challenge existing limits. Elon Musk, for example, is surpassing the public/private divide by entering into the former government-only domain of space research. He wants to change the way we look at the car as an instrument, or to reconfigure financial operations. He is a very good example of how technological development can have a powerful impact on politics or finance as well. The same can be said for the film industry. Or fashion. Almost a century ago, Coco Chanel changed the way society looked at women and men because she changed how clothing was perceived. So a fashion designer can have a big impact, a film director can have a big impact, and yes, an architect can still have a big impact. We can look at the impact of architecture on perception, and how architecture is dealing with technology. We defined the role and the position of the architect differently in the nineteenth and the twentieth centuries, and the way that we define it in the twenty-first, will be different, too. The architect's position is not only to create icons, but also to harness particular momentums for the society that is yet to be built.

> You seem to describe parallel momentums in modern society. How do you organize these parallel momentums for yourself, and how do you incorporate or bring them together as an architect in your work?

Arets: An architect always looks at the ordinary. There is a lot to discover when you open your eyes. It's not only about aesthetics; it's about seeing the possibilities. You can learn from what is happening in the streets of every village or every city in the world. As an architect, I'm very interested in determining how it is I can achieve something in an area where that was perhaps not possible twenty years ago. I have the responsibility to know what

WIEL ARETS ARCHITECTS, UTRECHT UNIVERSITY
LIBRARY, UTRECHT, THE NETHERLANDS, 2004.

will happen with the result, twenty, forty, or a hundred years from now. When we build a library, for example, I have to understand, what is this library producing for that particular city, for that particular client, and what can I contribute to the development of the library as a building type, or as a building that people are using in a slightly different way from how the library was used a hundred years ago? Also, how can that building contribute to the city and the environment; how can that building change or maybe anticipate new developments. In the case of a new museum, you know art is not static; it's changing every minute. So I ask myself, how can we make a building that develops new ways of communicating art to the audience? I'm extremely interested in architecture as a medium between the user and the product. Architecture allows us to artificially create the conditions in which people can flourish. The Allianz Headquarters, which we finished in late 2014, has about a hundred people working in an environment that may appear to be a kind of rough condition, but they have to search for ways to operate within it. That's also the task of an architect— to understand that when you create conditions that result in new behaviors, you also take a risk, change certain criteria, cross borders, and push limits. At the end of the day, it determines the success of the building. Everyone wants to see an office building, library, or museum that challenges the people who are using it. I refer to interiority. Not in the sense of the interior, but rather what you have in your mind; so the impressions you take home after you watch a movie, or see a work of art, which make you look differently at your home and the relationship you have with it. When I go to Africa or India, and I see people being extremely inventive in a certain condition, I learn from that. It's very important to be challenged and I think that architecture is a discipline that should enable people to feel challenged.

> While designing, how do you critique wheth-
> er or not your building is challenging?

Arets: For every design, I ask myself, what is the concept I would like to develop for this particular site for this particular client within these specific circumstances? Conceptually, you have to be as clear as possible on the one hand in terms of structural rooting, and incorporate ambiguity on the other, so that the building retains the ability to surprise. It's important to be able to act like a stranger in the building despite your familiarity with it, because a stranger is always asking questions. When people are challenged by a building over time, that's the product of an artist. Sometimes you use certain elements to achieve this. If you usually construct with a column or a wall, for example, you can also lead with a stair that brings you in, offers you a different movement, or a kind of interruption at key points. It's the same with a column—not every column in the building has to be the same. Columns can be bigger, or extremely small, or extremely fat. It should relate to the condition, and thinking about why we need a particular kind of column in a particular moment, in relationship to the overall concept of the building. As an architect, you have to ask yourself: what is the column, what is this column for, can this column do more than support; what is the wall, is this wall made in this material, does it have a particular color, or this kind of tactility? It's the same with glass, and steel, and the rooting: when I make a floor out of a certain material, I ask myself, what is the program of this building, does the floor have to be white or black, depending on the need for certain reflections of light? It's never as thoughtless as: we always make floors black or always make them red or white. A designer asks in each instance, why? A graphic designer may ask, why this paper? They don't use the same paper in every book, because they may want a photo to be exposed in a different way. When the book is thicker, the paper is slightly different than when the book is thinner; and that is what's happening in buildings, too. Sometimes a building needs lower or higher floor-to-ceiling heights, which is a decision you make based on the sequence: do people enter the building very low, and then enter into a bigger space, or do you do it the other way around, where they enter high and then transition to low? What is the program? How do you expect people in this building to communicate, with the building or with their friends, and how they can work in this building? If we painted the exterior of the Utrecht University Library [2004] black, it was because the material had a kind of three-dimensionality. A particular shade of black paint will change depending on the seasons: in winter, the building always looks grayish; sometimes it's white, or silver. So material, light, and acoustics work together. The feeling of softness when you look at a particular wall where the light is playing on it gives you a different perspective. In my opinion, the façade is something you can treat as a veil that has a kind of continuum, or perhaps just as a perforated surface. How you decide to treat it generates a tension between the aesthetics on the outside and the performance from the inside. Every architect responds to program and momentum and makes decisions slightly differently. Here at IIT, it is important for the students to understand that they are each communicating differently with each other and with this building.

How has your design process evolved against the broader context of the history of Modernism?
Arets: Though we are always children of our time, we also strive to be children of the time to come. To project forward, you have to be deliberate about the way you read history. History is not comprised of immutable truths: we all read history in our own way. As a student, when I made a decision to read a particular book, or to analyze a building, or watch a movie, I chose my influences.

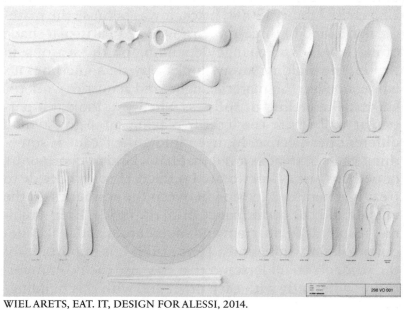

WIEL ARETS, EAT. IT, DESIGN FOR ALESSI, 2014.

Paul Valeri once talked about "the possibility to combine ideas." He meant that we make choices, and all the choices we make add up to our story. The world I am living in is based on the story I made from my choices. During and after my studies I traveled to Japan, the US, Russia, China, and within Europe. I made sure to look at the work of the Russian constructivists like Konstantin Melnikov, Italian architects like Giuseppe Terragni, Cesare Cattaneo, and Modernists like Le Corbusier, Mies, and Louis Kahn, but also Renaissance, Japanese, Indian, and Egyptian architecture. The real question is what my reading of them is, and how I think this history makes sense to me—that's what I tried to write about in my book *Wiel Arets: Autobiographical References* [Birkhäuser, 2012]. I mention, for example, that Villa Malaparte—a house Curzio Malaparte built for himself in Capri—had a big impact on my way of thinking because he was a writer who built a house, which he called, "a house like me." That implies that he is a writer who made a house whose design is based on his reading of his own history. Malaparte was the author of *La Pelle* [The Skin] and he was sent to the Russian front, of course, so he was a journalist too. He built his house on a cliff such that when you look at it, it is part of the cliff but it's an inside-outside condition. It has a flat roof with a kind of sail on which you can sit, and it had a fireplace which had a window to the outside which works like a kind of beacon for the fishermen. So how would architecture place that house, which is difficult to categorize? That made the house important for me. When you go to Hong Kong and see the walled city, a huge area that had became extremely dense over the course of a century, because of political conditions. 24,000 people were living there—it was an enclave or enclosed area that had an incredible impact on the way in which I understand the effects of building. So the only thing to do was to build denser and higher until it collapses under its own weight. It wasn't the product by an architect, but it's a circumstance I learned a great deal from. I can give you many examples of things I saw that others didn't see as architecture, which were the results of different impetuses, and helped me to understand my potentials as an architect. So the question is, whether we call it structuralism or modernism or whatever, I think you always have two components: one component is reading the state of our discipline. At any given moment there are always people out of step with a kind of slightly different reading, who are also doing great things. I am interested in those who are misreading or creating their own criteria and making a next step. All the "isms"—modernism, deconstructionism, structuralism—try to label what is at this very moment in the air. What is our time? That's one of the reasons why at IIT, I think it's important to have a kind of temperature reading. So we organized the Mies Crown Hall Americas Prize (MCHAP), which brings together projects of the Americas from the few last years into S. R. Crown Hall, and lets us debate what we think of them and what the world thinks American architecture is about. That's what we can do as an institution.

> Herman Hertzberger has often described architects as having a lack of trust for the public. But society, including architects, have also developed a growing trust in software. What might be the architectural implications of this?

Arets: Software is technology that we choose to believe in, not unlike an elevator that I believe will take me down, because it's been programmed to do so; or a car that I believe will stop when I push the brake, because it is made to do so. In a couple of years, yes, we will get in a car and we'll push a button and believe that this vehicle will take me somewhere because of all the software now making its way into cars. What's new about software is that we can't see it happen but we trust it anyway. With the typewriter it was physical—when you hit a key you saw it mark the paper. The whole idea of the unconscious is very important. I'm about to finish a book on the topic, which I started a couple of years ago, about the unconscious act where we are in a kind of flow state and the processes are invisible to us. But the physical, evidence, is still of great relevance. We trust physical reality: for example, our expectations for gravity to act on structures. The software can be used to challenge or bring people out of their comfort zones by inserting tension into their habits. So in the form of gravity defying structures, perhaps. I'm a soccer fan, and every year, there are players who do something more incredible. It's the same human being; they still have the same ball, and they still play on grass. But they are getting better and better, and that continues to interest me. I think that there is always a challenge to make the next step, and software is part of that. In a few years we will have software in our bodies. So the future will probably not belong to humans alone or robots alone, but rather some kind of relationship where we are enhancing our bodies, and our minds, with the help of the computer. But when we also produce something outside of ourselves, let's call it artificial intelligence, which becomes creative and will be able to repeat or copy itself, it will become a new a species that might engender some distrust. But I do believe we have to always challenge our discipline. And our changing relationship with software is one aspect of that.

> Under the framework of "Rethinking Metropolis," how would you describe your position on the future or trajectory of the metropolis, in the form of a sketch?

Arets: I think that the metropolis will be an area where we will have many different zero-levels. I think we will be able to be in an environment where we combine our current three-dimensional reality, with a fourth or fifth dimension. Especially when we are able to build with materials that are more or less transparent, and we are able to grow distinct microcosms within that. These environments will be interdependent, but also have distinct neighborhoods, which add up to the greater totality. I strongly believe that we will not live on one surface, with one ground. So where we now have the street level, on the one hand, we will also have possibilities for flying from one building to the other. Maybe in the years to come we will not make big distinctions anymore between the library and the theater as separate facilities, but rather as simply momenta where you go to charge, not only your car battery, but your own energy. So I think the most important word of the future will probably be energy. Energy for me—from the Latin, energia—is not only the thing we describe in a physical way, as in physics, but energy is also what Marcel Duchamp once said about painting: when you look at a painting, then this painting has a certain energy, and you are intrigued by the painting, and the painting can, during a particular time, create more and more energy. Then there's entropy, where it loses its interest, and maybe this will happen to the painting.

So the metropolis of the future, I believe, will be much more a kind of conglomerate, not completely flat, comprised of such momenta. What I like about Tokyo, for example, is that you have a city with these different neighborhoods, and you can go from one neighborhood to the other, and in each neighborhood you will always find everything you want. There is your subway stop, there is your hotel, there is your museum, there is your whatever—but there are still identities available to us. In the whole history of urbanism, whether it's Russian, as Nikolai Ladovsky's schemes, or Japanese, there's always a neighborhood thinking—a bunched-up city within another city. With all of these cities, these linear cities, it's not one city; it's always a city with varied momentum, here or there. So you can create something that is the same, but slightly different. Or, for instance, in the nineteenth century, with Ebenezer Howard, and these whole industrial areas where the city was a kind of core, which everything integral to it surrounded it. It's neighborhoods where you go from A to B; whether those distances are rather big, or quite small.

>Is that what fascinated you the first time you went to Tokyo?

Arets: Yes. And what fascinates me about Tokyo is that when you go to one of the many city districts you can find the smallest house, and it is probably similar to the smallest house you would find when you are a hundred kilometers from Tokyo. That house, in that small village, and the house in the center of Tokyo; one is in a neighborhood here and the other is in a neighborhood there. There's not such a big distinction in scale between cities and smaller villages, or towns, in Japan. Which is dissimilar to how it is here, in the United States.

FREEDOM
JUNYA ISHIGAMI

> You believe that a social project for architecture is impossible in the contemporary context, and that we must instead rethink a new relationship between architecture and the world. What is the evidence for your position?

Ishigami: I think that we had some unifying movement, or style, until about a hundred years ago. During that time, architects could propose the new society, the grand image of the future. But now we have no movement, at least not since the middle of the twentieth century. We can't decide on one future, and each person has a different style. So architects have to propose another type of style and solution. So I think that the important thing to note about the moment architects are in now, is that they do not make just one solution. I want to think about how to create a different kind of architecture, without architecture.

> Does technology play the role of style today? In other words, does technology help you identify the work that is produced and for whom?

Ishigami: I think that style means something different for kings, the masses, and everyone in between. Everything has a style. Technology is the wrong term to relate to contemporary architecture. It used to be that function was the most important element of architecture, and under fixed conditions, the function could be fixed as well. Conversely, under changing conditions, we have always shifted the meaning or the function. For example, if a client asks us to do an office building, but later there is a change in the client, the function probably changes too. I think that's an important part of any architecture. The function is important, but I think we have to think about another relation, another way of thinking about buildings than form follows function. I'm not interested in a temporary building, I'm very interested in how a building becomes history.

> You once said that, "The responsibility of an architect is to have a perspective that goes beyond the scope of human beings." In your opinion, what is more important than how humans inhabit buildings?

Ishigami: Of course I think a building is for human beings. At the same time, we have to think about a wider audience. I think that the twentieth century was about cities, because the scale of the architecture impacted the scale of the city. Now I think the city-scale is too small for the kind of architecture still to come. The city is an artificial, constructed environment, and we have to think about natural environments as well, because human beings influence the natural environment. That means that the natural environment is a kind of a mixture between human-made, artificial environments and natural ones. So I think we have to take a more global view, meaning that a building is not just for human beings, but for other species as well.

> What would you say is the responsibility of an architect?

Ishigami: I think the responsibility of the architect is how to treat the architecture, because human lifestyles are always changing. For example, forty years ago the human house was completely different, compared to the house of today. That is the kind of responsibility of the architect, to constantly think about new types of space to fit domestic lifestyles.

> You have said that our everyday interaction with our smart phones has given us a new sense of autonomy in space. How can design respond to this far-reaching social change?

Ishigami: The modern condition, as measured in the speed of building, but also the speed at which we develop new electronic devices, is completely different than in the past. The cycle of electronic devices being produced and becoming obsolete is extremely rapid. At the same time, the time needed to build a building is really long. I think this gap is very important. Electronic devices are always changing, and architecture is also changing, but architecture will remain far into the future. So architecture is a kind of environment. Electronic devices are an activity. We do have to think about how to introduce new technologies into the building, but at the same time, knowing how to reject that new technology is also important for architecture. Just including everything is not good for architecture. Some rejection is also important.

> You've described society as being somewhat elusive, and as result you are interested in proposing a certain level of ambiguity or what you call "freeness" in architecture. How do you incorporate this ambiguity into design?

Ishigami: Historically, we had much less access to information than we do today, so it was perhaps easier to draw a line around an architectural movement. Today nobody seems to recognize what is a real thing, what is not important, or what is important. So a true understanding of reality lies is recognizing all the information that is available, in other words, the ambiguity of the metropolis. I think the borders between things are very ambiguous.

JUNYA ISHIGAMI, CURVES VISITOR CENTER, PARK
GROOT VIJVERSBURG, THE NETHERLANDS, 2010.

> Is social life today as complex as the natural environment or climatic phenomena? How does your use of environmental references aim to create an architecture that responds to the current condition?

Ishigami: This is related to the previous question. I think that today, nature is not just natural form, but includes the human activity that is transforming the natural environment. So we have to consider how to mix these two aspects, natural and non-natural. Originally, human beings made buildings to be comfortable in the space inside. But today we can't decide what a natural environment is, and what is a human environment is. That means that we will probably have to rethink what territory means, too. Before, we could very clearly divide nature and our architectural environments, but now the architecture environment and the natural environments are becoming blurred; we cannot divide them so clearly.

> You reference cloud-like experiences in your architecture. What attributes of clouds or the atmosphere do you think are useful in creating architecture?

Ishigami: It's not just the form, and not just the cloud, but the cloud as a kind of metaphor also. I think a cloud has a shape, but at the same time, a cloud is also a phenomenon that is constantly changing. But they sometimes keep their shapes. I like that.

> Your research on animal behaviors has also influenced your work. How do you create an environment that bases human social life on natural organic principles?

Ishigami: In reality it's very difficult, but also possible, to make a building not just for humans but also for animals.

I want to think about how to advance the biodiversity of the natural environment while keeping the architectural environment, and how to connect this environment to the surrounding environment. I think that context is very important. Normally, architects make a building in the city, in which case the context is about the kind of the history, or the kind of relationship with the neighboring building. But if we make a building in the middle of nature, we have to reflect on the existing environment to find context.

> Many of your projects have a "natural" relationship with structural ideas, in which you disrupt the normal perception of gravity. How does this advance your idea of ambiguity?

Ishigami: For me, the structure and the ornament of a building are equally important. I want to think equally about the whole of any building. That means that whole elements have some kind of structure, even furniture. Gravity is important for architecture, but it is only one of the elements that condition the building. It is sometimes very important in some projects, but the most important point, for me, is the existing condition of the site, or the existing condition of the space or environment. The existing condition of an environment also makes a building.

> It could be said that you produce a different tectonics. Your tectonic expression seems to search for the zero degree of minimalism, in terms of the size of the columns, for instance.

Ishigami: Yes, and I also think, that the existing environment automatically makes a new type of building.

> Why do so many practitioners of architecture in Japan integrate structure, art, architecture,

and history? Why do they come together so easily, in Japan?

Ishigami: I don't know. I grew up in Japan, so I am heavily influenced by Japanese culture. Naturally. I think the delicate sensibility of the Japanese arts has probably had an influence on me.

> You seem to be interested in finding a way to design space free of geometry or rules, which could possibly lead to a new notion of universal in space. How does your technique construct universality?

Ishigami: I'm always finding random geometry. So I think that random things can become good structure, but they are also very difficult to make for human beings. For example, if we insert a lot of trees into the landscape, freely, then automatically the trees become aligned in some sense. Probably, it's very difficult to make a truly random project. So, I want to think about how to do free geometry.

> How do you make your decisions then, if it's not based on geometry and rules?

Ishigami: A program does not automatically make a plan. That is a kind of support for the design. Architects have to decide everything. So of course, in a normal building the decisions of the architect are very clear. I want to make columns, walls, and other architectural elements ambiguous. Of course, architects have to set everything up. But at the same time, I want to make the units ambiguous, because I want to incorporate some flexibility in buildings. I don't want to divide elements. I want to see the whole elements of architecture, complete. The important thing is how you connect each element, or treat the local relationships between elements. That is very important to me.

JUNYA ISHIGAMI, KANAGAWA INSTITUTE OF
TECHNOLOGY WORKSHOP, ATSUGI, JAPAN, 2010.
INTERIOR VIEW SHOWING LOCAL RELATION-
SHIPS BETWEEN STRUCTURAL ELEMENTS AND
FURNITURE.

In other words, you are challenging architecture to create new propositions that could transform the entire value system of architecture?

Ishigami: I'm looking for a lot of variation to the solutions in architecture; that is my challenge. So not just one way; not just one direction. Because today, everyone is so unique. Variations are needed to support this diversity of people.

What is your approach to teaching architecture?

Ishigami: Teaching trains you to think about the different ways that architecture can be made. But whether I am teaching or working in my studio, the important thing is to make architecture. I want to make an environment. Not just a space, or a structure, but an environment.

STEFANO BOERI

While you may be described as having any number of careers, from urban planner, researcher, professor, and intellectual, to architect, the most surprising was your failed campaign for mayor of Milan. Given the contrast in cultural priorities between designers and politicians, what expertise were you hoping to bring into that sphere?

Boeri: A politician, whether in politics or public policy, is basically dealing with space—the changes that occur in space with the creation of new conditions, such as the introduction of barriers or fences, or the potential to reuse space or the significance of space. Whether my position has been as a designer, teacher, magazine director, or politician, I have used it predominantly to address space and its potential to influence or condition the behavior of people. That has been the core focus in all of my activities. So, I consider myself an architect, first and foremost, even though my role is often found inside other disciplines. In my opinion, an architect's role is about anticipating the future of a specific space, and at the same time hosting inside us what is normally totally contradictory. We have to be extremely open, or inclusive, on one hand, and absorb the complexity of reality by accepting information, data, comments, documents, and voices. On the other hand, an architect must act to reduce this complexity as well; we must select from the possibilities of the future by defining one unique and singular physical configuration. Not two, not ten, not one hundred, just one. Being an architect means we must simultaneously combine the capacity to be inclusive with the necessity to be selective and exclusive. The schizophrenic cohabitation of both approaches is something that enables architects, whether we are acting as politicians, magazine directors, teachers, or researchers, to intrinsically remain architects.

> Starting with the research agency that you founded, Multiplicity, you often investigate territorial transformations in areas with very specific political conditions, such as Tehran and Belgrade. What is the relevance to the field?

Boeri: I always try to confront existing approaches to investigation and, at the same time, define a methodology of investigation. What has always been quite particular in our experience is that we are asked to "broadcast" the methodology of our research together with the results. This answers the question of falsifiability or fabrication of the research. There are two ways of exhibiting a research project: the first involves an investigation, whether on Belgrade, Tehran, or Istanbul, of which the results are broadcast as a series of images or as a finished project. The second type of research requires an additional discussion on methods, approaches, and perspectives used in different contexts. The second path puts the public, the visitor, or the reader in a position where they are capable of evaluating—or falsifying—not simply the result, but also the approach or method. That is the contemporary relevance—having your failures pointed out so you may learn from them. With respect to relevance at the time, when I first started working as an architect, it was still a small world, and people were opening up windows on geopolitics and geographic environment that had been simply forgotten. This includes work at the Berlage Institute with your own Vedran [Mimica] at the end of the 1980s, or our own work with Multiplicity in the early-1990s. Now, I think it is a completely different scene.

Is one of those examples of early research Catherine David's Documenta X exhibition in Kassel [1997], which was a critical examination of the political, cultural, and economic challenges of globalization?

Boeri: Yes, Catherine produced an amazing exhibition. Part of it was looking at different models of urbanism in the postcolonial context. She had invited Rem Koolhaas to talk about China and the Pearl River Delta, and I had been invited to talk about Multiplicity. It was an amazing moment in which the art field was more critically aware of what we, as architects, were doing, than we were of what other fields were doing.

In the architectural field we had basically completely isolated ourselves at the time. At the end of the 1990s, architectural discourse revolved around styles; it was a self-focused discussion between urban forms, programmatic planning, and deconstructivism, that was not able to find its role in the contemporary geopolitical scene into which architecture is inserted.

As a member of "the Tomorrow / New Narrative for Europe" project [exhibited at the 2014 Venice Architecture Biennale, you argued that Europe is simply a very large polycentric city, populated by thousands of small and medium-sized urban areas. What is the status of the project today?

Boeri: As researchers, we often talk about Europe by observing its geography and the state of things: how people move or feel, how the new generation of European students experience places, and how one can travel from one part of Europe to another in one day. Studying these conditions instigated our *USE—Uncertain States of Europe* [Skira, 2003] research, first published in *Mutations* [Actar, 2000]. But this is not enough, because you have

"VOTE BOERI" ADVERTISEMENT FOR THE
PRIMARY ELECTION FOR THE MAYOR OF MILAN,
THE PRIMARIES, 2011.

to repeat the exercise as designers to prove its feasibility. Near the end of our research, we designed a map of Europe using the code of a subway map, but at the scale of a continent instead of a city. The map was simply a visual graphic. However, the implications behind the design were more profound. We discovered from the map that Europe takes the form of a city with many centers—it is a common urban environment composed of thousands of small to midsize cities that share the same conditions.

Regarding your question, New Narrative for Europe is moving forward—it was just approved by Jean-Claude Juncker, the new president of the European Commission, even though, in all honesty, it was a failure. After we produced all of the research, the results indicated that we should try a new narrative. But every narrative we proposed reduced the project to a mess. Consequently, we entirely rejected narrative as an organizing genre, and instead proposed a conversation. Our position was, what gives Europe its identity will always be a conversation. This is self-evident in our work with the Tomorrow [thetomorrow.net], which instigates email conversations about Europe through a public web platform. We chose the medium of letter-writing because it is very important to the DNA of Europe. As a tool, it closely resembles European intellectuals' historical mode of exchange—every thinker from Plato, Goethe, and Schopenhauer, to Freud and Einstein communicated through letters, so the Tomorrow is an attempt to continue an epistolary tradition.

> The European Union has made political statements on achieving social and urban sustainability for all EU territory by 2050, under the Environment Action Program to 2020. Do you believe these can aid your own vision for Europe?

Boeri: The question ought to be, what is a political European policy? Europe is an archipelago where the plurality of subjects, in terms of language and culture, is irreducible. At the same time, the various islands within this archipelago share the same seas, oceans, and lands, causing highly specific but common conditions across them. Starting with such complex, differentiated territory challenges every single attempt at policymaking in Europe; things have to change from one country to another, or one region to another. Even within nation-states you find political requests for independence, for example, in northern Italy, or the Catalonia region in Spain, or with the Scottish referendum in the UK, or even popular nationalist movements, such as the far right in France. So EU political statements are at risk of failure immediately.

In this context, the environmental issue could become a crucial one, but only if it mirrors a spectrum of issues. Sustainability, in my view, is not only about how to implement and gather renewable energies; it also has to deal with de-mineralization of urban surfaces, such as the extension of green roofs, facades, gardens, parks, and so on, and with biodiversity—the cohabitation of different species inside an urban environment.

In your essay, "Architecture is/as Politics," you assert that architects possess an excess of knowledge, and most architectural research is wasted as a result. Why do you see excess research as wasted, and given your position, how do you suggest it could be redeployed?

Boeri: Let me elaborate on the dangers of excessive research first. There is always a risk that one will try to use all of the results of the research in their design approach; there are many architects that complicate their design approach in order to retain the richness of the information they have accumulated as researchers. These architects are so self-referential that their work is extremely repetitive, and ignores content entirely. There are other architects who are so aware of and open to the changes in their context that they are constantly changing their approach. They allow the complexity of reality to confuse their design solution. Naturally, there will be structural weaknesses in the design because all hierarchies are transient. These are two instances of the misuse of research. Now, to answer the question you actually asked—in my opinion, architecture is forever producing an excess of knowledge to which the political sphere does not pay any attention. That is a pity, because architectural research is useful for any number of disciplines. It works on the surface of the world, looking for clues that are symptomatic of larger-scale phenomena occurring below the surface. It relies on the architect's ability to detect what is invisible from an excess of information. I would go so far as to argue that in the recent history of the city, architects have understood and foreseen structural processes that many politicians or others in the political sphere were either not able to see or did not have the courage to confront.

Can you give specific examples of that?
Boeri: At the 2015 Venice Architecture Biennale [curated by Alejandro Aravena] there was great interest in informal settlements. Now, architects started researching informal settlements twenty years ago. That was the first wave of thinking about the issue. With our São Paulo Calling research [2012; 2014] we acknowledged that an informal settlement was not simply a common condition, the same everywhere, but a complex condition with several differences manifesting across settlements. As the research evolved into thinking about the highly specialized, productive activities hosted by these settlements, architects were able to bring to light that informal settlements are not simply a place for the poor to reside. They were something

STEFANO BOERI ARCHITETTI, BOSCO VERTICALE
(VERTICAL FOREST), MILAN, ITALY, 2014. VIEW OF
"BOTANICAL CLIMBERS" PRUNING THE FACADE.
THE MAINTENANCE PROCESS WAS DOCUMENTED
IN THE 2015 FILM, THE FLYING GARDENERS, BY
THE BLINK FISH.

different—places that were actually producing wealth. Architectural research undertaken on informal settlements in São Paulo and Mumbai, for example, were eventually considered extremely fertile material for politicians to use. This is just one example, there are countless others.

> A final question about geopolitics, specifically your Solid Sea project. In Solid Sea 01: Ghost Ship, which you spoke about at Documenta XI in 2002, you were the first to show refugees drowning in the Mediterranean, and highlighted the contiguity of routes between European and African shores. The project offered a strong political message that doesn't seem to have resonated with politicians. Why do you think this is?

Boeri: This relates back to your query about excess knowledge. Why is it that our politicians do not consider this excess knowledge? This is a perfect example of useful knowledge being disregarded. At that moment in 2002, migration flows were not particularly relevant, but we were there to witness the tragedy and use it to highlight the greater relevance of the issue. This information was produced by architects, and was an example of the changes in political conditions around the Mediterranean Basin, yet unfortunately, it has not been considered, even with the recent crisis of Syrian and Libyan refugees.

> In your book, *The Anti-City* [L'anticittà, Editori Laterza, 2011], you describe it as a "fragmenting [of] the urban society" caused by a "dissipation of urban energies." How can architects operate in this paradigm? Furthermore, do you believe this is a condition which should be resisted?

Boeri: It's a good question. The "Anti-city" is always the dark side in the city's folds. Its ingredients are not easily defined, because it is comprised of a variety of spaces. Each enclave manifests a different condition of modernity, and different social behaviors, with invisible barriers between them. We could better define what Anti-city is if we started with what I consider to be the basic character of a city, which is intensity. Intensity is produced by the combination of a density of spaces, with a variety of cultures and social behaviors. When you don't have one of these two characters, or both, the Anti-city grows. The point is that without a relevant variety of cultures or languages, and a strong density of spaces and landscapes, the city won't have the necessary richness in which we all want to live.

> Rem Koolhaas famously commented that "people can inhabit anything. And they can be miserable in anything and ecstatic in anything. More and more I think that architecture has nothing to do with it. Of course, that's both liberating and alarming." Do you agree with this statement?

Boeri: I read it as Rem's realization that the general condition of architecture often does not have the capacity to produce excess or extreme conditions. In other words, architecture is condemned to produce mediocrity or forgettable conditions, instead of unforgettable excesses. If we observe the professional standard of most architects, Rem is probably right. That is why it is much more interesting to observe the happenings of social life itself rather than the happenings in the spaces architects are producing. And that's the reason for our research on Tehran or Belgrade; the information, details, and clues that can be extracted from these niches of reality are far richer than what can be extracted from a set of "well done" architectural proposals. This was the fundamental insight that lead to the commencement of *Multiplicity*—the new is not necessarily inside architecture. Sometimes, the new can be found as much in self-organizing processes that change space, giving us reason to observe places once thought to lie outside the realm of architecture. That's my interpretation of Rem.

> You wrote a "manifesto" on the new localism, which appears to be a kind of compendium of observations. Do you believe that localism is still important at a time when the dominant ideology is globalization?

Boeri: In my opinion, localism is still relevant, but only from one side. The localisms referred to in the manifesto are not proposed as miniature globalisms, but localism as in "the eye of the needle." In other words, they act as a sort of threshold through which a thread of transformation must necessarily pass. That is to say, global flows are running everywhere, but find different kinds of resistance in different local environments.

We must ensure that we do not isolate local spaces from these global flows, and simultaneously, we must observe how these global flows are always conditioned by what is local, that is, the physical and symbolic condition of a specific location. We used the term "Glocal" to demonstrate how, when acting in a local condition, care must be taken with regards to global processes; it is not an implicit opposition to globalization but rather calls attention to the process by which the constant flow of information starts running through a location. Every part of its components should be deciphered and analysed in order to see how its parts are changed.

> As the editor of two Italian magazines, *Domus* and *Abitare*, you consistently represented architecture's successes. Yet, you decided at IIT to introduce an alternative narrative of archi-

COVER OF ABITARE MAGAZINE, SPECIAL ISSUE
45+1, ITALIAN OXYGEN, NO 488, DECEMBER 2008.
CHIEF EDITOR: STEFANO BOERI.

tecture through its failures. Why this provocation, at this time, in this building?

Boeri: I do not believe this kind of provocation has been considered alongside history. It's crazy, but architects typically do not talk about failures, flops, or collapses. Architecture lectures are always about a sequence of victories, which is unbelievably stupid. We, as architects, do not use mistakes to improve the quality of our work; we should view failures as materials to strengthen our capacity to change the reality. This lack of consideration is very specific to architecture. Generally, when a consideration is given to a profession's failures, it is a very serious point. Look at the air crash investigation industry, for example. I have yet to see any evidence of this in architecture, a sort of black box for architecture. It's a failure in failure—a tautological condition.

At the Chicago Architecture Biennial, you presented a short film, *The Flying Gardeners*, describing the extraordinary work of the "botanical climbers," who maintain and prune the approximately 900 trees of your Bosco Verticale project in Milan. Was the film meant to document a failure of your architecture?

Boeri: [Laughs] I don't know! It's just documenting the reality. I was very attracted by this completely new profession, in which botanists have to become climbers, or climbers become botanists, as a consequence of the architecture. For me, the film was simply a way to talk about the building, but from the perspective of the people taking care of its maintenance. I do not really think of it as confirmation of a failure. In what way do you consider it a failure?

Perhaps the building's excessively high need for maintenance?

Boeri: That was a decision that was made during the project. We discussed whether to give to owners the possibility to maintain their own balconies. However, it was decided that we would centralize the maintenance, for various reasons. The flying gardeners would prune the plants from the exterior twice a year, while the rest of the maintenance occurs from inside the apartments. The decision guarantees good maintenance, yet, at the same time, provides some prerogative to project an image of public gardens. I think it was the right decision.

> As a professor at the Polytechnic University in Milan, and a visiting professor at a number of other universities, what do you see as lacking in architectural education?

Boeri: I don't know if it's possible to define only one uniform condition of weakness. What one would consider lacking in a Chinese university system is different to what one would consider as lacking in a European or American university system. It's a very important question, but not easy to answer. In my opinion, a portion of a student's curriculum should always be inside a professional firm in which they are undertaking professional activities. Another position is that any student, at a given time, ought to be put in a position to teach. As a teacher, I can honestly say we always learn a great deal from our students. It is true that students are not conditioned to understand that every time they speak up, they are indeed teaching. What I attempt to educate my students about it is that they can be their own teachers as well. When they research, they should understand the results as other possible answers to architectural problems. However, as I said, it is a difficult question to answer without taking into account the different conditions and contexts of different universities. The Anglo-Saxon model is totally different from the Latin or Italian models. In China, there is also a completely different understanding between teachers and students in the field of architecture.

> Your mother, Cini Boeri, is also a well-known architect and designer. Could you talk about how this, and your family in general, have informed your architectural education?

Boeri: My mother is now ninety-two and still works! Her profession as an architect and designer has always been a very important presence in my life, although I have never ostensibly collaborated with her. Well, we had one experience: we designed a small house in Switzerland together in 1985–1986, but it was a disaster. She was, and still is, so strong-minded that I really had to do my best just to be a part of the design solution. In the end, the result was horrifying. It was not a synthesis of two different approaches, but more a superimposition of the two. My father was a neurologist and I learned a lot from him as well. The point is not about having a father or a mother who is an architect to aid your education in the field; both my mother's and my father's professions have aided my architectural thinking. My father, especially in relation to psychology and physiology, was much more helpful for understanding the relationship between social behavior and physical spaces. Whereas my mother, who was basically a furniture designer that did two or three amazing houses, was obviously important to my design thinking. Now I have a son who is starting his studies in architecture. He is doing the same thing I did with my mother—he doesn't want to talk to me about it. But what's important is he knows that the door is open.

AUTHORITY
PETER EISENMAN

You distinguish between a project and a practice by arguing that while a "project defines the world, practice is defined by the world." Yet, haven't powerful practices shaped the world?

Eisenman: I believe that there are two avenues to power in architecture. One is through design; the other is through the intellect—that is, thinking. When I finished school in the United States in the 1950s, I thought that power was gained through design, and so my models were Le Corbusier and Mies van der Rohe. I went to work with Walter Gropius because I thought he was a designer—it turned out he was not a designer. After six months I left and met James Stirling, and showed him my work. He said to me, "Peter, you are a really good designer, but you don't know anything about architecture." Which was true—I was innocent. Jim advised me to be with Colin Rowe at Cambridge, in order to learn about architecture. Being with Colin Rowe for three years, I learned about the other power: the knowledge of the discipline. It was a very important lesson, that power in architecture can also come from knowledge, just as much as design. I am convinced that all the students can design well. But can they also think? If there is anything a school can give students, it should be the capacity to think. Practice can only become powerful if you can think and have knowledge of the discipline, which is gained in the studio, not from history classes. Studio is also about teaching project, namely, the power of ideas. Some of that involves going to the library. That's how

you teach—by reading and thinking in the design studio; you can't just have a history-theory sequence. That
is why it is important to have a library in S. R. Crown
Hall; integrating theory and history into studio is the
way to achieve a powerful practice.

> The question was not about how one can have
> a powerful practice, but how a powerful prac-
> tice defines the world.

Eisenman: At the present time, most practices in the
world are power practices that don't have a project.
There is not a single Mies or Adolf Loos among them. So
in order to attain the kind of power you refer to, project and practice must be integrated in a studio, which
isn't the norm in most schools. I remember when I was a
student at Cornell, one of my teachers was Romaldo Gi-
urgola [1920–2016]. Perhaps he is not known anymore,
but he was an important Italian architect. Every Friday
morning, I was in his 9:00 a.m. class, having returned
from party night on Thursdays. He hardly spoke any English, and I didn't really care either, because the class
wasn't a studio. But I appreciated that he was teaching us project. Until we bring projects into the studio
as an attitude, we will not have power, because a practice doesn't ever become powerful by itself. I don't know
any architect who has power that does not have a project; their practice often becomes powerful through that
project. Rem Koolhaas, Rafael Moneo, Tadao Ando, and
Oswald Mathias Ungers all understood that, and they
had a project. Gropius had a powerful practice but not a
powerful project, and therefore he will be less when we
discuss Mies, Corbu, Frank Lloyd Wright, and Loos. To
me, Bjarke Ingels is not powerful at all. He's just an en-
trepreneur. There is a big difference between Ingels and
Koolhaas, and that difference is important.

But do people like Bjarke Ingels have some
kind of authority, because of their practice?

Eisenman: Bjarke Ingels is so successful because his clients do not want an authority, which speaks to the times
we are in. That's the trouble with our society—we no longer have the need for authority. We want crowd funding
and bottom-up thinking instead. What kind of surgeon
would ask his client about how he should operate? What
kind of lawyer would ask a client which way to argue
a case? What writer would ask the readers to tell him
how and what to write? So why should an architect listen to bottom-up opinions? When authority is no longer looked upon with respect, we end up with someone
like Donald Trump in public office. He, as a developer,
builds inferior buildings and hires mediocre architects.
He doesn't care about the project at all; he just wants to
make money! Not only is he a person without morals,
he is a person without scruples. He is emblematic of our
time, which is why I don't want practice to be powerful.
I want projects to be powerful. Radical Italian thinkers
like Bramante, Brunelleschi, and Borromini were powerful because of their ideas. Do you think that anybody
would care about Robert Venturi's practice if he hadn't
written *Complexity and Contradiction* [The Museum of
Modern Art, 1966]? Or, that anybody would care about
Palladio's modest villas if he hadn't written the *Quattro
Libri* [Dominico de' Francheschi, 1570]? I have always
stated that books last longer than buildings.

How relevant do you think a project can be
without being practiced?

Eisenman: Manfredo Tafuri once told me that nobody
will care what you think, if you don't build. Conversely,
he also told me that if you don't think, nobody will care
what you build. That is so important to understand. We
are currently doing the construction documentation for

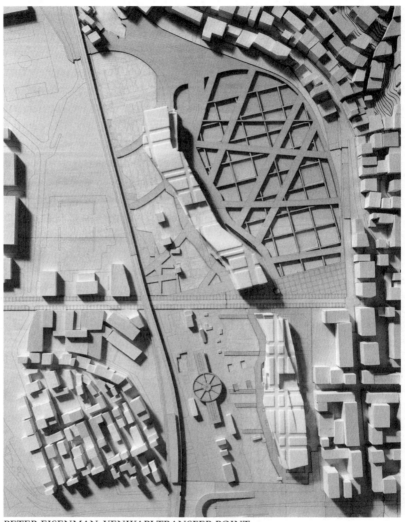

PETER EISENMAN, YENIKAPI TRANSFER POINT
AND ARCHEO-PARK, ISTANBUL, TURKEY.
PLAN VIEW OF ARCHITECTURAL MODEL.

a 450,000 square-foot museum in Istanbul, the Yenikapi Museum, and I've realized how lucky I am: at the age of eighty-five I am doing a big museum, I have just finished two books, and I'm teaching. I am doing exactly what I think an architect should do, which is to do both. In other words, it would be a mistake to stop practicing and concentrate solely on a project. Since most people in this world are practicing without a project, however, my recommendation would be to worry about projects more than practice, as it is easier to go into practice than it is to have a project.

> Do your clients defer to your authority, and what compromises, if any, do they make when they choose to work with you?

Eisenman: My clients know the difference between Peter Eisenman and Frank Gehry, although Frank has many buildings and I do not. I believe that clients generally don't want architects with projects. I think that a project is a contradiction to practice, which is why it's so difficult to do both; they stand opposed. Frank has a great practice, but less of a project. I believe that I have a good project but less of a practice, which is why I am excited to do a large museum like Yenikapi. I don't get my projects from clients; I get them from competitions. One of the marks of an architect with a project is an architect shunned by clients. I can't tell a client why they should build a project, because they would not understand. A client often hasn't a clue why we do what we do—but that is not important, as long as the architect understands, any client who chooses to work with me, compromises. Doing something that the client wants is compromising. Last week we changed something on the east façade of the Yenikapi museum, and the client said to me, "Peter, you have 600 drawings and the changes you wish to make will change a hundred drawings! We are hoping to go out to bid tomorrow, do you still want to do drawings or do you want to go out to bid?" That is my compromise: the east façade is not going to be how I want it to be. I still want to tweak things and the clients want to build! What's interesting about this client is that they have never set us a budget, allowing us to draw them what we wanted. So the compromises are coming. At my stage of life, I want to see the building built. I am less interested in the 600 drawings that are going into the archive.

Can you define your projects?

Eisenman: No, that's for you to do. I don't need to, because I do it. I am not an historian. I can define Koolhaas's projects, or Moneo's projects, but I can't define mine.

In projects such as the City of Culture at Santiago de Compostela, or the Yenikapi Museum in Istanbul, you interpret ideas from the site that you arbitrarily use to generate the figure. Can you talk about the notion of the arbitrary in your work?

Eisenman: When the ideas are from a site, they are no longer arbitrary. So I object to the term arbitrary. Unless you are arguing that the site has no relation to the building. Moneo always argues that my work is arbitrary—my response is always a disagreement. The module for the Yenikapi project comes from the modulation of the Hagia Sophia, which we discovered in our studies. No one from the city administration knows that, but it is clearly identified in the grid, and so it is not arbitrary at all. The former harbor walls of the site were used to define the figure, so the building is long as a result. The building takes the form of the old harbor, whose archaeological ships it houses. You might think that's arbitrary, but I cannot think of a better way to do it. So I stand categorically opposed to the arbitrary.

In a panel discussion with Preston Scott Cohen where you spoke about the superimposed grids in Santiago, you said yourself at one point that it is arbitrary to some degree.

Eisenman: Let's take the example of this table. Why is this table this shape in this room? Is it arbitrary? No. Would it be an equally effective table in this space if it were square? I don't know. So I think a degree of arbitrariness plays a role in everything we do, where there is no extreme logic being applied. Speaking of the arbitrary, have you asked Rem why the CCTV is the shape it is? I know why; I did a building in Berlin in that shape. It's that shape because it was against phallocentric architecture. Phallogocentrism, which was a strong feminist idea from the 1980s and 1990s, made us decide that we shouldn't be building phallic symbols anymore. We had female architects working with us, and we thought that there should be other kinds of tall buildings. So we made a Möbius strip, which can never be interpreted as a phallus, as it is always twisting in on itself. However, my client died, so the building didn't go ahead. Yet I am still wondering about the shape of the tower. It is an important question. But none of my projects, whether they're in Istanbul or Berlin, are arbitrary—they're absolutely thought out and related to the site.

You talk about the idea of lateness, both as a critical moment in time and a late moment in your practice. Are you trying to evaluate your project in relation to the conditions of the present zeitgeist?

Eisenman: Beethoven wrote the Missa Solemnis a few years before his death. If you look at the Missa Solemnis, it is completely different. It is argued that the Missa Solemnis was Beethoven's late moment—that is to say, it is a piece that breaks away from the work that had led him toward the nine symphonies. Had he lived beyond the Missa Solemnis, I believe he would have done something different. I am eighty-five. I am already playing against time. So what can I do? I read Edward Said's book, *On Late Style* [Bloomsbury, 2007]—"late style" was the phrase Theodor Adorno used to describe Beethoven's third—because I am trying to find out what my late being is. I am in "late style," whether I like it or not. You cannot do things until you die, because we have to put a capstone on our existence. I don't think I am eighty-five, but I am! I have to keep up with young people; with their energy and ideas. It should be said that I am out of touch with the present zeitgeist: the millennial project, crowd-sourcing, and object-oriented ontology are not my game. I am not interested in many things that being worked out in the present, since there is nothing that I can teach of the present. I have recently completed a Palladio book, and I am working on an Alberti book, for which I learn something new every time I give a lecture. I just reread an article by Rudolf Wittkower, about Alberti written in 1938. It's a fantastic article with a different view on Alberti. But I can't teach Jeanne Gang or Zaha Hadid, and parametric software, because I wouldn't know how to; nor would I want to. So instead I teach Alberti and Bramante, and I take my students to Vigevano [Piazza Ducale] by Bramante. To me it is the best square in the entire world. There is a church there by the Polish cardinal, Juan Caramuel y Lobkowitz [1606–1682], which has a facade with four openings. The fourth opening is where the cars and secular people enter from, while the other three are standard entrances into the church. Massimo Scolari wrote a book on Lobkowitz, *Oblique Drawing* [MIT Press, 2012], as he was both a Polish cardinal and a practicing architect. I cannot talk about today, because I am still learning about yesterday!

You have predicted an epistemic paradigm shift in the next twenty years, which will create space for the development of a new "meta-project." What do you believe will drive that shift?

Eisenman: I can't answer futurist questions. I believe that there will be a paradigm shift, but I don't know what it will be or what will drive the shift. I am not sure, but it is not global warming. That will happen and we will deal with it, but that is not going to be the main driver of the architectural shift. To be honest, I don't think democratic capitalism, as a project, works anymore. It cannot afford security, healthcare, or sustain infrastructure. Capital, as a system for politics and economics, is on its way out. Towns like Flint, Michigan, don't even have money to purify their own water. What worries me is that we could see more authoritarian politics and economics, which will be a real problem. Don't forget, the major built accomplishments of the modern movement occurred during and against periods of fascism, communism, and Nazism. In other words; repressive authoritarian governments. So it could happen again. I can't tell you any more than that, but we will probably see a shift in the socio-political economic structure that will affect architecture in a big way.

In your opinion, what will be the three buildings that Peter Eisenman will be known for?

Eisenman: I would argue that the most known project would be the Berlin Holocaust Memorial. It is a complete outlier that has more to do with my practice and little to do with my project, yet it will exist for 500 years. The same could be said for the University of Phoenix Stadium. It is in the public eye and everybody knows of it. To me, however, they are not my project. For me, the most important projects are Santiago de Compostela, the University of Cincinnati Arnoff Center, and Wexner

PETER EISENMAN, CITY OF CULTURE, GALICIA,
SPAIN, 2011.

Center, or any one of the house series—probably House II, as it has a more theoretical development than any of the others. The CCA in Montreal has over 300 of my development drawings for that house. Just the other day, I had a very sad moment because some people in Vermont wanted to buy and save the house, but they needed to raise $350,000 to do so, which was not possible. House II dealt with the dialogue between the column and wall, which is an Albertian project. Alberti said that the column is not structural but a residue of the wall. The project followed the idea that the columns are not structural, rather the walls are. The columns were ornamental. This was not the case for any of my other projects; the theoretical message is very much tied to Albertian theory. For me, the didactic nature of that house is very important. The client was an American nihilist-communist who was in Hanoi during the Vietnam War when I did his house. He told me he had hired me because he wanted me to do a Chomsky project. He came back and visited the house with his wife, who said, "Oh my god, I thought we were getting a Heidi house." They wouldn't live in it, so they built a kitchen and bathroom in the basement and lived there instead, in protest of the house. It was great, because the house itself was a protest, but against middle-class and bourgeois values. Jeff Kipnis has just written a great book, *By Other Means* [Global Art Affairs, 2016], where he talks about the conflict within myself: I'm the prototypical American bourgeois kid, who runs into philosophical discourse and fights against himself, for which there is a struggle and an eventual return to my original values. It is a beautiful essay that's absolutely true. It was published in the Palazzo Bembo at the 2016 Venice Architecture Biennale.

A few years ago at the Berlage Institute, you presented on a conversation you had with

Jacques Derrida, and why you saw him as an idealist. You went on to mention that architecture couldn't exist without idealism. Could you elaborate?

Eisenman: Rosalind Krauss wrote an essay called "Death of a Hermeneutic Phantom," in which she writes that modernist sculpture and painting really are more radical than modernist architecture. In her opinion, modernist architecture wanted to idealize technology, structure, new materials, and new social ideas—it was the continuation of a Kantian project of the late-eighteenth century. All of the early-nineteenth and twentieth century architects whom we admire had this idealist streak that remains unacknowledged. This condition is the hermeneutic phantom of modern architecture, according to Rosalind Krauss, when she talked about the unspoken idealism of modern architecture. This project of idealizing new techniques and materials did not have the radicality of modern painters and sculptors, because it didn't aim to estrange or defamiliarize, as they did. So I would argue, as Derrida did, for the moral idealization of philosophy. Namely, the deconstruction of ideas. I would say Derrida was a moralist and an idealist; Jeff was ultimately saying what I was too. Students should understand what that means, or at least make sense of it as an open problem, as it's the latent idealism—in terms of modern architecture—we teach in schools.

I wonder if you could expand on your intriguing analysis of Giuseppe Terragni in your dissertation, *The Formal Basis of Modern Architecture* [Lars Müller, 2006]?

Eisenman: I was travelling with Colin Rowe in 1961, and had been given a book six months earlier, by Sir Colin St John Wilson [1922–2007]. In the book was the Terragni building. I said to Colin, "We've got to go see this." So we left Bernhard Hoesli, who was then dean of the ETH, and drove from Zurich to Como. Colin used to tell the story that when we came upon this certain square in Como, I had had an apocalyptic revelation. I had never seen a building like that, and even now I still see it as amazing. When you come upon this white half-cube in the sunlight, it is incredible. So, I decided I wanted to write my thesis partly on this building. It was really important to me, even though I had never wanted to be a teacher; I had always wanted to be an architect. Eventually I wrote my dissertation at Cambridge. I could never do another book quite like that one; there were hundreds of drawings. Rem used to say to me, "You and Terragni are both B-movie architects." I would say to him, "Well, I love being a B-movie architect, because I love B-movies." But I don't think about Terragni anymore. I have never taught Terragni. *Ten Canonical Buildings: 1950-2000* [Rizzoli, 2008] came out of a class that I taught, but it was Koolhaas, Libeskind, Moneo, and so on. Terragni was a moment in my life that I am not in it anymore. I am not sure know how you would teach Terragni in today's climate, anyway.

> What was the importance to the New York Five?

Eisenman: The problem with *Five Architects* [Oxford University Press, 1975] was my inability to be me, in it. I was always inventing new institutions and projects that I could appear within, such as the Institute of Architectural and Urban Studies (IAUS), the Conference of Architects for the Study of the Environment (CASE), and P3. With The Five Architects, I didn't know what I was doing it for. It began when I went over to see George Wittenborn, who had published the first edition, and told him that I had the tapes from a meeting we had had at MOMA, CASE 7, and 8, which was also the basis for *Five Archi-*

tects [Wittenborn, 1975]. I had been ready to announce the book with the title *Cardboard Architecture*, which was the title of my essay, but the group said, "No! That was not our idea, we can't call the book that." When I asked them what they would like the book to be called, they said, "We don't want it to be called anything! We don't like each other, we just happen to be doing this book together." After that, we just named it, "Eisenman, Graves, Gwathmey, Hejduk, and Meier." The final title came from Paul Goldberger, who published a story about the book calling it "The New York Five." We had nothing to do with each other. We were all very different. We published 500 copies of the original book, as we were not very interested in its publicity. All we wanted was to make a nice book, and it turned into an ideology. Getting out from under the association with The New York Five was difficult for me. That's another period of time, like the Terragni period, I'm always trying to get away from.

What is the book you want to be remembered for?

Eisenman: I haven't written that book yet. Venturi's *Complexity and Contradiction* was the first book of American theoretical architecture practice. Rem's *Delirious New York* [Oxford University Press, 1978] is a very important book and will be remembered long after any of his buildings. I haven't written the book I want to be remembered for, yet. I don't know what it will be about, but that is my late project. It's not Palladio, Alberti, *Ten Canonical Buildings*, Terragni, or *The Formal Basis*.

When will this book come out?

Eisenman: I am still trying to understand what it will be about. It could be about anything, even soccer! I once did a book, *Contropiede* [Skira, 2005], which is Italian for counterattack. They bring the enemy very close and then they attack with their libero, or their defensive players. I took the term and published a book. I think that I'll do something very unique. When I work with students, or when I work in my office, I want to do something that no one else does. I don't know how to theorize what that will be, but nobody that I know, understands what it is.

ETHICS
RAFAEL VIÑOLY

Your career has had two very distinct chapters:
first in Argentina as the Estudio de Arquitec-
tura, and later in America as Rafael Viñoly Architects. How have these two environments
shaped your architecture?

Viñoly: I moved to America in 1979 for political reasons.
I had knowingly worked for a very repressive regime, and
I woke up one morning and realized I was becoming part
of it too. I couldn't stand that idea, so I left that very day.
At the time, I had an office of 150 people, which was a
very large operation for South America. I thought that
I already knew everything there was to know and that I
was fully prepared. The reality was very different when I
landed in New York. I had to figure out everything from
how public transportation works to getting on a bus and
not knowing what the person next to me was trying to
tell me, and whether they were friendly or hostile. It was
a fast-paced, phenomenal learning curve, which every
immigrant has to undertake. I also refused to retreat into
the protective shield of academia, as others in my position might have done. I had one fundamental concern
on my mind, and that was to start building. It was very
tough, but it has been the best thing I've ever done. It
trained me to understand diversity. There is an assump-
tion people make about globalization that everyone can
work everywhere, which I don't really believe is the case.
There is always friction. The most important thing you
need to handle the diversity of varied environments is
the strength of mind to interpret your position within
the discipline. You can only bring something to a dif-

ferent place if you have a central rudder that is organizing your work. Once you have that, then you can benefit from multiple environments.

> How does your built work translate into pedagogy?

Viñoly: Nobody defines what architecture is but you. I have been teaching for a long time—I formed an independent school in South America, and I've taught at Harvard. There is no single method of architecture that can be taught, we can only try to hone the qualities that everybody has, which are intelligence and the capacity to think strategically. Of course, you also need to learn that the profession is subject to a number of external pressures that exist independently of you. Architecture has always experienced peaks and valleys, which touches on what the changing role of the architect is over time, and whether we are fully subservient to technical conditions or to more abstract forces. If you look at the composition of the profession now, it is basically divided into these two extremes; they are polar opposites on a band of possibilities, which unfortunately diminishes any chance of occupying the middle ground. But architecture also occupies the only media that you cannot turn off. You can choose not to attend a concert, or to close a book, but you cannot avoid the built environment. Being here in S. R. Crown Hall, day after day, it affects your DNA, I can assure you of that.

> In a previous interview, you mentioned the importance of having a "process of self-criticism" in order to find your own method or approach to architecture. What is your process?

Viñoly: Self-criticism is so important because it is the only tool we have as intellectuals to try and understand what it is that we are trying to do. If I don't know how to do something, or if I don't know whether an option is good or bad, how can I, as an architect, identify the multiple paths forward in order to choose the best one? It's not about conducting a moral inquisition, but rather having the capacity to thoughtfully inquire. By the time you leave your house every morning, you have made design choices, such as which set of clothes to wear. With a little self-reflection, you can even choose whether to be happy or unhappy that day. So self-criticism is learning that you can choose, and that your ability to choose can be trained up. It's the fundamental mechanism for any intellectual life. None of us are on a linear track of development in the modern era. The choices to be made in everyone's life are unbelievably varied. I use the word "choice" here to mean the ability to take swerves from the conventional, assumed, or expected path, not the consumerist sense of choice.

Ethics, responsibility, and strategy are a big part of your lexicon. Why?

Viñoly: It's crucial to have a sense of ethics; the basic principles on which we base our choices—whether they are harmful or beneficial, and for whom—are the essence of what ethics are. Ethics, by this definition, undergird your architectural vision. Again, it is not about being moralistic, it's so much more than that. You cannot disregard the public effects of the objects that we produce. Take the 1980s, for example: during this period, pleasure and self-satisfaction were the twin forces driving postmodernism. The sentiment was that if you like something, why don't you just do it? If you like Italian balconies, why not just do it here in Illinois? I remember having a conversation with Susan Sontag in Denver around 1985, in which she said she perceived postmodernism as a social phenomenon that had to be at some level concerned with the ethics [of seeing]. What I took

RAFAEL VIÑOLY, 432 PARK AVENUE, NEW YORK
CITY, NEW YORK, 2015.

from that is that architecture is like photography: it creates and condenses our relation to the world, so that ethically, it is important what you choose to photograph, or in this case, build, because you are imposing your preferences on the rest of society. Postmodernism, as it has been practiced in architecture, enables you alter the consciousness of the residents on a surface level without actually contributing to the public realm and altering society in a larger sense. Planning, as a discipline, has also completely missed that regulatory aspect of design. There are some ideas out there about light and health, but there should be a trillion more ideas than that. In the recent past of what's been called "planning," it wasn't actually planning, it's just architecture at a very large scale. To me, the creation and the development of an ethical sense needs to occur at every level.

> What then is your social agenda? Are there any projects of yours that you think particularly embody this agenda?

Viñoly: I try to pay attention to the public implications of all of my projects. Although that doesn't mean much these days. The world has changed. Twenty years ago, the notion of the public realm was a hippie, leftist idea operating in the shadows. Now, it's what all architects do. They cannot survive if they do not make a presentation to a room of 700 people who mostly have ill-informed opinions about architecture. And that's standard now for how we all must work.

> Is this why your work shows a preference for the large scale?

Viñoly: To use a musical metaphor, if you asked Mahler to write a duet for a viola and a cello, he could not do it. He would need something like 164 musicians to do anything, because his mastery lay in the large form.

What I'm saying is, some people work better at different scales. I don't think that scale determines how your career plays out, but you may start with the tiniest jobs, like your aunt's kitchen, and then move on to bigger things. Now, it would be hard to describe the public dimensions of your aunt's kitchen, right? But at a certain moment, when you have to design the kitchen, you have to ask yourself what the relevant properties of the kitchen are to you, and these lessons carry with you. Architecture is more than an aesthetic or an observational exercise—it's about executing your own purpose. It used to be a given that the design choices of the architect would influence the philosophical or pedagogical approach of the institution the building houses. This notion of purpose appears largely absent in today's world. When Mies did S. R. Crown Hall, there was a notion that function could shift the neutrality of the institution through the idea of technology. This has actually come to pass. What is Big Data, but a way of assuming that the rules governing society can be predicted and guided by the analysis of large sums of data? Data points today are selected for use in the studio in the same way that a person would select from a paint palette for a painting. But like every technology, it is simply a tool, albeit an extraordinary one.

What do you believe to be the most pressing problem in the field today?

Viñoly: One thing that is becoming obvious to everybody today is the tension between the individual and the collective, which is exactly what the founding fathers addressed in the United States Constitution. [Alexis de] Tocqueville also wrote about the collective in the form of voluntary associations. It is generally a good thing when you and sixteen other people are operating to create a collective effect, but when the group is much bigger, the collective impact of any activity can be extremely varied.

So if you design something with a narrow view of the building as an object, you are missing that dimension entirely. The best architecture is not looking for a spectacular momentary effect, but is actually concerned with redefining the problem. This can be seen here in S. R. Crown Hall, which is something that Mies invented. He not only reinvented neoclassicism, but he also invented the relationship between the different parts in the building. Yes, he was a great detailer. But this is a 100 percent pure architecture. You don't last as long as Mies has if you're not a real architect.

Is architecture becoming irrelevant as a consequence?

Viñoly: The world around us that shapes the profession forces everyone into one of two camps: the design architects, of which there are few, and the architectural producers, of which there are many. The problem lies with the producers who get student interns to produce these renderings of wacky designs for their clients at an unbelievable pace. In between, not only is there no architecture, but there is also no architect. An architect is a person who intervenes in the physical environment at every turn. If Mies hadn't detailed S. R. Crown Hall the way he did, this space wouldn't be what it is. This approach is lost today and that is the fault of the profession. So with all due respect to students, I have concluded that we have a gigantic vacuum. It's lovely to teach you all and see the students so interested in the subject matter, but the problem began long before you got here. The physical environment, as a fundamental level of human activity, should be taught starting in grammar school. It should inform children's choices as they begin to develop a way of life that suits them. You can only realize a high level of complexity in your architecture when you understand the elementary things: the aspects of the material envi-

RAFAEL VIÑOLY, 432 PARK AVENUE, NEW YORK
CITY, NEW YORK, 2015.

ronment that hurt or improve your life. I am currently trying to convince a group of donors to create a program in Europe, New York City, and Panama City that can be implemented in a chain of elementary schools.

How do you teach children about the physical environment? Can you give us an example?
Viñoly: I went to a school in Panama for three days to teach architecture, and it was completely improvised. There were approximately forty-five students, aged seven to twelve. The first day, I asked them very simple questions, like whether the room was large or small. Then I asked, large or small in relation to what? How can I establish what is considered large? This is a simple notion, but a very important one—the room we are in could be probably the size of a large bedroom, a medium sized conference room, or a very small theater. That idea of size doesn't exist until you know part of the program for the space. The second day, I told the kids to pretend that we were standing in a glass courtyard and that they owned one side of the plaza, and I owned the other side. Both of us were allowed to paint our own side any color. Suppose I painted it all in red, would that be OK with them? Red is the national color of Panama, so of course they said yes. When I asked if I could paint it yellow, which is the color of Colombia, everybody said no. Fundamentally, this is about the separation between public and private, which is exactly what architects do. So for the first time, they saw the problem of shared space and the implications of private ownership for each party. Now, if you extrapolate that, the discussion of what constitutes publicness is at the root of all politics, and the rights and duties of ownership and relationships between owners are manifested in cities as physical form. An architect must stop to think for at least five minutes and realize that they have a choice to be an instrument

or a critic of these conditions. The fact is that nobody knows anything about architecture and don't notice it until they realize that it affects them.

> Was exposing this choice an explicit goal in your design for the Tokyo International Forum [1996]?

Viñoly: When I did the Tokyo International Forum, I won simply because of the public plaza I had incorporated between the atrium and the buildings. Everybody said it was the most normal thing in the world. There were subway stations to the north and south, so why should people have to go around the building instead of being propelled through? The interstitial space was large enough to put two or three bars in there, and you could rest under some trees if you wanted. Yet the first thing they did when the building was built was to put in a gate. It lasted a week before they realized they had to remove it. Later, I did the Jazz at Lincoln Center [2004], and I always say that jazz is the purest American art form that exists—not only because it is diverse, but also because there is nothing written, it begins with improvisation. The Tokyo plaza is understood through improvisation too, that's why it works so well.

> Many of your skyscraper forms seem to be generated with rent/profit-maximization in mind—your Walkie-Talkie tower [20 Fenchurch Street] in London, with its bulging upper floors is one example—so how do you negotiate between your commitment to the client and to the public?

Viñoly: It is not about commitment to a client, because the developer doesn't even know about it. In London, a tall building is considered to be thirty-five stories, which is a nonsensical misinterpretation of what a tall building is. As an architect, you know that isn't a tall build-ing, because a tall building is, let's say 1500 feet, and you know that what is vitally important in tall buildings is the relationship between the form and the technology. But all the other proposals were standard extrusions of the site with a thinning of the tower at the top. They believed they had to make the top thinner because the project was framed by the rhetoric of a tall building. I told them that it was clearly not a tall building. It's only a thirty-seven story commercial tower. So eventually I proposed a scheme that was shorter but more profitable, and the developer just looked at me and said, well, that's great. But this is only anecdotal. What I'm trying to tell you is that you don't need to convince anybody if you understand the game, and the real game on that project was to expand the public contribution by placing a pub-lic park at the top of the tower. This is what made it work for the public, the authorities, and the developers.

> Speaking of tall buildings, 432 Park Avenue is the tallest residential skyscraper in the world, made economically viable by the value of land in Manhattan. What lessons have you learned from this project that might be applied else-where?

Viñoly: The client had acquired the site many years ago and had wanted to do the building for a long time, but they did not know how to solve the structure, or under-stand the possibilities of the zoning window and nav-igate the various regulatory and planning agencies in Manhattan. New York City is the ultimate vertical city because it is on an island, and cannot grow horizon-tally. So the zoning regulations require setbacks at vari-ous heights for reasons of public health that can quickly make the project financially unfeasible. Part of it was fig-uring out the envelope in which you can build and what the massing should look like based on views to the sky. You also have to respect the client's price point—if they want to make 18 percent profit, that is what you have to design for. Lastly, the process of architecture is so complicated and fragmented today, that we have lost much of our scope to an expanding number of consultancies and overseers, such as production architect, design manager, project executive, and we wanted to regain some of that. So those were the constraints.

For the massing, we were interested in working with proportion. Also, a question was: who are we going to sell to? The program was luxury retail, hotel, residential, and in the process of defining the proper mix of program, we settled on a mix of one to two apartments per floor in the fifty-four upper floors of the tower for a total of a 104 luxury apartments. We also wanted to redefine luxury for New York City with 14-foot clear ceilings. I would say the lessons for structure were extremely important. Because the building did not have a large footprint, we wanted the structure to be stiffer, and dispersed the wind effect by breaking it up into six vertically-stacked buildings. We went on to do structural basket mock-ups for the window panes and designed the sash system for deeply recessed, square windows. We always tried to use our own expertise to make ethical choices for the client.

To give an example, at first it seemed like our clearance requirements would mean an expensive poured-in-place concrete stair. So it was up to us to argue that we could use a prefabricated scissor stair to save money. These are things only the architect who knows what he or she is doing can say. The engineer can only tell you how many square feet of concrete you need to have in the ground floor. Whereas the interior designer is a specialist in sinks and fabrics and doesn't care where the pipes are. I didn't have to work hard to convince the client to do anything because we were making the best choices, and that it how is should be.

TECHNIQUE
BEN VAN BERKEL

> Do you believe it's necessary to advance your ideas through both building and writing?

Van Berkel: It's important to find ways to reflect back on your built work, and to develop strategies that help you discover something new about it. I believe that you can do that through writing, where you ping-pong between your work and your writing, so that together they mobilize your thoughts and concepts into prolific new directions. Sometimes this means you have a theory about the work up-front; at other times you create an after-theory.

> How do you achieve balance between practice and reflection, writing and building?

Van Berkel: Balance can often be found in the way that one filters teaching through practice and vice-versa. Academic time is much needed for the research side of practice. Although teaching is one model, I've found others too—I read a lot, I have friends who are in different fields, and I draw and paint also. I've learned over the years that there are many ways to reflect back onto the world.

> Your publication *Move* [with Caroline Bos, 1999] was an early reflection on how you re-imagined your studio and approach to the profession. You claimed that "[t]he architect is going to be the fashion designer of the future." Why was that an important moment for rethinking the role of the architect?

Van Berkel: *Move* was my first publication about the tools of the architect. The most essential part of the book for me was the middle, where I reflect on the idea of what tools can do for the architect's imagination. We have a tendency in the field to believe that if you have a vision, that's all you need to project a design or urban plan into the future. But I discovered—perhaps because of my research in science and detailed observations of how artists work—that artists were far more experimental than architects with techniques. They would draw over a silkscreen technique and re-photograph it, and then silkscreen it again. They made double use of context. These techniques gave me new ideas about how to stimulate the imagination of the architect. We typically view the architect as someone who provides a practical political or social solution for a highly specific condition at the behest of a client, whereas in the role of the architect you can also generate your own brief, or twist the brief to suit an architectural agenda. That's why Move was such an important opportunity to reformulate the practice.

> Did *Move* also help you develop the idea of the architect as the orchestrator of a group of professionals from different practices?

Van Berkel: That way of working existed for me before Move—I often invited my friends from the movie or fashion industries to the studio. There's this amazing trend forecaster, Lidewij Edelkoort, who is often hired by designers. She predicts things like what the future of fashion and color will be, and how we will drive or live differently, and she is often spot on. I once consulted with her for several weeks on a book. As I watched her work from the studio, I discovered that she read almost twelve newspapers a day. Then she would pick out a topic, like the Pope's visit to Latin America, and analyze how the articles in each paper were written with a different political message about the visit. She'd try to find all the different ways that information was being presented, politically and socially. It gave me so much insight into how we as architects can think, and this was before we had social media!

> Although Ms. Edelkoort immerses herself in knowledge, wouldn't you say that fashion isn't really a research-based practice?

Van Berkel: It's not just knowledge, she brings in an argument or story. She sees the world of theater in the world of fashion, and shows us that it is not superficial or one-dimensional. She gave me a lot of inspiration. I've been interested for a long time in social science and anthropology, and I still read a lot on that topic. It's very important to understand what is happening in other fields in terms of invention: what kinds of inventions, how do they occur, and what kinds of techniques are used? That's why my story about Lidewij Edelkoort is significant; there are lessons—where does she invent, and how does she predict a future that's impossible to predict, because after all, who can predict the future? She tries. As architects, we need to do that too.

> Where does invention or the process of innovation take place in your studio?

Van Berkel: It takes place in our knowledge platforms, which are basically networks of internal and external specialists that we've set up. These specialists are invited to contribute to a material platform, or a parametric platform, for instance, which could also overlap. It's an unusual system of collaboration. On the one hand, these platforms are about achieving efficiency and more compact communication. But on the other, they're about trying to combine or cross-fertilize information from each specialist within the community. They can make you go in totally unexpected directions during the work process.

Do you think that the knowledge platform is a good model for all architectural firms in the future?

Van Berkel: It's difficult to say that because every firm has its own method of working, just like artists do. Some offices do have a separate research division. What I can say is that, in the future we must bring insights about the new forms of complex regulation that exist into the work and to structure that process. When you come to the contract phase of the design process for example, that model is so mixed up right now, we have to be careful that we are not guided by the contractors or the developers, and instead develop our own models. It's necessary for practice to further expand on that.

In the diagram of the knowledge platform where many ideas are working together and given equal weight, how do you judge, or make the decision to move forward with one?

Van Berkel: It's not crystal clear to me. I should explain our workshop model further: we have all these different workshops within the project, and then we invite different platform members to be part of the workshop related to a very specific topic. We did a project for the Fraunhofer Institute [a virtual engineering company in Stuttgart] a few years ago that was a prototype for the way they believed people were going to work in their office structure in the future. Since we were not allowed to call it an office building or office spaces anymore, but rather laboratory spaces, we mixed everyone in our office who had previously worked on office spaces before with others who had designed laboratory buildings. This drew out ideas on how a laboratory environment could be applied to the organization of an office building. So that's how we structure the workshops, bringing in people to exchange information with one another to ensure that we've captured all the logical and experimental possibilities for a project.

> If, as you seem to be saying, it's left to the process to determine what takes priority, couldn't individual platform members bias the decision in one direction or another simply by speaking up more often or more eloquently?

Van Berkel: No, I'm very careful about that! I make sure that everyone learns to be part of the process. Of course, some information is more important, but I'm the one who guides that determination. I invite everyone in, and sometimes I will even select interns and who is going to say what at a given moment. Sometimes there is an open moment in which to speak up, or I will just say, "show me what you've prepared."

> Working at the intersection of disciplines seems to be a specific interest for you. Could you elaborate on this interest and on the scale at which such interventions take place, from object to city?

Van Berkel: When I talk about the cross-fertilization of knowledge, I'm also talking about the many overlapping structures and systems in a design that are without scale. It's more about the proportioning of information than of scales. You can serially deploy a strategy that works in a small-scale project or a large-scale project—that principle or larger detail could be tested over numerous projects. The idea of the "twist" for instance, I've tested over several projects at different, overlapping scales.

> Does that become more interesting when infrastructure, typology, and disciplines are also overlapping?

Van Berkel: Yes, exactly. I test principles for what is typo-

UNSTUDIO, MOBIUS HOUSE, HET GOOI, THE
NETHERLANDS, 1998.

logically possible, and try to invent new typologies like the laboratory-office building or the museum-department store. These hybrid possibilities for programmatic exchange also come out of the physical organizational properties of the project. It's the play between the physical organization of the building and the programmatic fusion that I try to introduce.

> It seems like in many of your projects there's a similar duality at work, for example, between infrastructure and program, or between motion and occupation. Would you agree?

Van Berkel: It's not a simple thesis, antithesis model. It's richer than that. I'm interested in creating another form of experience. I'm particularly interested in the notion of the afterimage. If some kind of ambiguity is to be found in the work, then it has to do with perception and experience, or rethinking the work by going back to it through the idea of the afterimage or afterthought. With an afterimage, projects can become thought models. It is very important to me that the project is not based on a single ideological or conceptual argument, but rather that it is layered.

> What role does technology play in producing the thought model?

Van Berkel: Do you know the book *Objectivity* [Zone Books, 2007] by Peter Galison? I read it five years ago. It's about the emergence of "objectivity" as a concept in the nineteenth century—how it came out of new technological instruments, particularly the camera, that were invented to help us understand nature. I often look at the development in history of techniques of drawing or image-making to copy nature, and I think about how technology can influence our understanding of nature. Technological invention has always been a social complement to our existence. We've developed and expanded our social system through technological ideas. I've always believed that technology is incredibly important and can stimulate the profession. Sometimes we are not aware enough of it.

>Does technology help you develop more experiential effects in your projects as well?

Van Berkel: Yes. Architects used to like technology so much before, especially when we talked about high-tech architecture. We liked to point at where the technology was to be found. I don't do that so much. For us, technology stimulates the form of a new experience, like new forms of foils in glass or new ideas of reflectiveness. Yes, these are technological inventions but they give a different effect from the original principle when we start to experiment with it.

>Are those effects driven by technology or by aesthetics?

Van Berkel: Neither. It's the play between them that produces something else. I'm less interested in aesthetics, more in cultural effects.

>You mentioned that Sigmund Freud and Gustav Klimt were in critique of each other—although maybe one more than the other. Do you see your work as a critique of today's scientific knowledge?

Van Berkel: I appreciate a lot of the innovation going on at the moment. It's more than in previous eras. I'm especially fascinated by the computational advances we're making. There are also some really wonderful developments in medical science, or energy storage. But we need new understandings of science. When we talk about objectivity today, it's a most difficult topic, because what is objective? We can't agree on what is truthful and correct anymore, and what objectivity means. Peter Galison [author of *Objectivity*] defines it as a "trained judgement." I almost started to believe that with trained judgement we could arrive at a single way for how to talk about design. You have to be collectively trained in order to judge the right solution and move forward to the next phase of the design. Galison also did a movie on secrecy. It's a fairly new topic that is on the one hand, scientific, but also part politics, social communication, and social science. He is on the fringe of the scientific world because he invents his own topics. People like him fascinate me the most when it comes to how one can set up a critical dialogue between science and innovation, and the world of architecture and design.

> You mention technology, computation, and science, but not the innovations of architecture. How do you further the discipline of architecture with these innovations?

Van Berkel: I try to be critical about how we use computational strategies in architecture. I think it needs to be argued through the history of architecture and science. But with respect to what the computational can do for architecture, I'm afraid that if we use the computational as a way to develop only little segments within the profession, then it's not really helping the profession.

> You've used the terms "post-parameter" and "post-parametric." Could you expand on those?

Van Berkel: Parametric design relates to how you mix the logistics of information; it comes from hybridized, combinatorial organizational strategies. This doesn't mean that it's advisable to talk about how the layers of information can support the theoretical side of architecture, or about the specific intelligence of one parameter in the organization of the parametric. That is not doing

UNSTUDIO, ARNHEM CENTRAL TRANSFER
HALL, ARNHEM, THE NETHERLANDS, 2015.
VIEW THROUGH TWISTING COLUMN-ROOF
STRUCTURE ONTO THE LEVEL BELOW.

anything for the content of design. In my opinion, parametric design has been useful for comprehending the organization of a network structure, from that knowledge, I can derive things like the complex meshwork structure or overlapping cloud structure. But from a purely aesthetic point-of-view, parametric fields are not so important. How the knowledge and intelligence behind them gives you new forms of inspiration is. I think we need new ideas on how to go beyond the parametric as an infrastructural tool for design.

> You often note that advanced technologies allow architects to design much faster, produce more models per day, and communicate efficiently with clients. How has the new speed of production changed architecture?

Van Berkel: One of the most fascinating aspects of our culture right now is that you're expected to produce fast, but often you don't know why you're producing so quickly. Before you know it, you're just following the ambitions of the client who wants you to be commercially efficient, in order to earn more money as quickly as possible. I turn these contextual ambitions into a design advantage by trying to radically select what I choose to work on. This brings back some control over the process, not in the traditional master-architect sense, but in the opportunity to edit, select, and be a bit more critical during the different phases of design. And quickness can be an enormous advantage in that you get through your ideas much faster. If you choose to do larger details for example, that is a very good way to be compact and quick while working with major principles in architecture.

> Your design for the Scotts Tower in Singapore, a modular structure with large details, seems to reflect this speed of design?

Van Berkel: The modular is an endlessly relevant topic. Take the example of the Möbius house. I introduced only three angles—7 degrees, 9 degrees, and 11 degrees— that dictate how that highly complex geometry came together. There was a logistical reasoning at work. The angles were selected for the way it could be built with a particular kind of process and pre-casting technique. But, I also started to bring in the idea of how you can proportion geometrical elements for the way you experience them. The Möbius house looks quite complex, but when you start to move through it, it's serene. The reason is these three elements, and how they repeat themselves. It's almost like the logic of music, which induces an unexpected calm. I wanted to liberate any kind of stylistic reference in the architecture by introducing a transformative experience that was geometrical in form. The Möbius House was where I discovered that the modular does not only provide an advantage in the production process, but leads to an enormous number of new spatial and organizational experiences as well.

So the Möbius House is just the same module three times in?

Van Berkel: Yes, but the section is so diverse that it allows for a series of other complexities to emerge from within. This is the difference between talking about scientific critique and scientific discoveries. In architecture, we like to reduce. I'm both experimenting with that principle of the reductive, as well as what can be unfolded instead of reduced. So maybe there is an attempt to instrumentalize the way you experience space. If you go from an idea to a form then your work is concerned with the representation of a strategy in design, and that is what can be questioned, I think. Why should one work with that classical notion of representing form when you can work on the instrumental aspect of spatial experiences?

Are competitions a part of your model? You once mentioned that you prefer not to win the competitions you do because it gives you a chance to rethink.

Van Berkel: I use the competition as a way to experiment or test. I can tell you about a recent competition we did for a museum. I had the initial thought that art fairs are far more fascinating than museums today. Art fairs are comparable to the classical salon, where art collectors came together to consult about the latest work they bought, or what they could buy, and the prices. It's a bit of a marketplace like the salon used to be, where all the work was hanging on the walls and artists and collectors would fight about the quality of the work on the walls. I wished that the museum was like that again. So could the museum be a fair? Would the client work with that? I can talk about it because we lost that competition. Sometimes it's better to do ten competitions a year because then when you lose one it isn't so difficult, and you can use them as experiments. So don't do three competitions a year, because then it feels really bad if you lose them.

What did the judges think of it?

Van Berkel: They liked the idea but they didn't like the building. The problems with juries—and I'm in them myself all the time—is that if one person starts a conversation in a bad mood, then it spreads around the whole room.

Our new cloud studio at IIT is based on speculating about the city, its conditions, building types, and lifestyles of the future. Do you have a position on the future or trajectory of the metropolis?

Van Berkel: The classical notion of the metropolis is a very old model for the way we look at cities. I'm not sure

UNSTUDIO, VILLA NM, NEW YORK CITY
(UPSTATE), NEW YORK, 2007.

we can still talk about the metropole today as a place with its own identity and infrastructural origin. A city like Los Angeles had original characteristics, but that is changing. There is a lot of complex knowledge to consider, so I don't have many new ideas, but let's try to find out what the new city is going to be like. What could we name it instead of just "city," and how could we give it a new form of intelligence? The metropole, as described in various manifestos in the history of architecture, comes from a modernist, industrial history of the city. I think we should move away from that industrial model and find a more contemporary model. Although you don't want to solely embrace the development of ideas around the "smart city," there is something to be learned about how we can connect the city differently, and document it differently than ever before, and I find that it has not been studied well enough.

> In our studio, we focus on mapping the city to understand contemporary urban conditions and systems. We look for places to intervene, where there's an overlapping issue or scenario that we could then program or engage with. Do you have any thoughts on this process?

Engineers have researched so many advanced new technologies and computational techniques. They can measure the heat within the city or the effect of the landscape in the city. Perhaps we should bring them in to tell us things like heat levels within the city, or the effects of landscape in the city, that we have the ability to measure today. If we want to make the city healthier for instance, that's one topic. That's exactly were the parametric goes wrong. You have to think beyond it.

There is a great need to improve cities today. Take China, they are really looking for new solutions to reduce the use of cars in cities. In Huang Zhou, where

I'm currently working, my client is hoping that with extensive programming we can induce some people to stay for longer than a week on the site. That is scary on one hand, but on the other hand it's quite fascinating to see these ideas now being developed by certain clients and politicians.

> Do you think working in China is helping you develop urban strategies?

Van Berkel: We did some research around Penn Station in the start of 2000 (or the end of the 1990s) where we used a strategy called "deep-planning." It was a first attempt to cross-combine engineering or technological innovations that are found in the city. Over the years, we've been able to implement that research in our urban strategies. It's quite amazing how intensively I used that Penn Station model for other projects. For instance, I now apply knowledge of user groups and infrastructural management of people flows to my buildings to avoid congestion. A certain building can even accommodate almost 10,000 people in a day. So again, there's my fascination for the way one can learn from infrastructural knowledge and apply it to programmatic knowledge.

> How do you make the leap from gathering a pile of data on the city to an architectural design solution?

Van Berkel: Often the best thing to do is find an organizational strategy first that supports many different urban qualities. The way that Manhattan originally operated is a beautiful example, where the goods were coming out on the edge of Manhattan through the piers. Consumption, production, and high finance were all connected to the edge of Manhattan. The grid itself wasn't so important, rather, it was the way the grid was working as a machine for production and high finance. That's why Manhattan became so successful, and the model of Manhattan was copied so often.

> Your diagrams of the Penn Station added a temporal dimension to Manhattan, by taking time and usage into account. You said that new way of representing Manhattan helped convince the politicians of its importance.

Van Berkel: Yes, that was interesting because city engineers had never seen their own data visualized. They had only looked at numbers. They were perplexed by how much program could be found around Grand Central Station. Through visualization, they suddenly saw this twenty-four-hour cycle at the location, which proved to be one of the most active locations in the city. Then I told them that Penn Station is the opposite. Because if you come out of Madison Square Garden at 8:00 or 9:00 p.m., then it's as dead as the worst place in Manhattan, and they couldn't believe that either. They had it in their data but they had never seen the data in that way. That is what I find most fascinating—not particularly data, because that is not my fascination, but the way you can find techniques to communicate information more easily. Knowledge needs to be visualized, reinterpreted, and edited constantly through visual communication techniques. That's a very different topic altogether, but perhaps it's the key to how knowledge should be deployed by the architect.

PEZO VON ELLRICHSHAUSEN

One of our main research themes here at IIT is "Rethinking the Metropolis." How do you see your work in relation to this context?

Pezo: This is a well-intended challenge. I suppose referring to a metropolitan dimension is about understanding architecture as part of a wider context. But this dimension should not only imply the size and scale of cities, but also the multiplicity of events that take place in them at the same time. Instead of the metropolitan, I find greater challenge in the cosmopolitan condition and its density of diverse lifestyles, which can certainly affect the way we think about and produce a work of architecture.

So the cosmopolitan condition affects your architecture?

Pezo: On a conceptual level, I would say it does. Even if we live far away from that compressed diversity, we are inevitably aware of it. At a practical level, I don't really think so. In fact, we have done only a few projects in urban contexts, and for a limited range of programs. Of course, our life is significantly influenced by our many trips, and by our experiences in different geographical or cultural contexts. But there is nothing explicitly cosmopolitan in the buildings we have made. Perhaps our approach already contains a position towards civic or social problems. We might be intuitively transferring what we see to what we do.

Sofia: We have voluntarily chosen to live and practice from the periphery, or from the edge of what might be considered the cultural epicentres. Our vision is therefore predisposed to that angle, by looking from a distance, from a rather diffuse, selective and partial view. Borges, the great Argentinian writer, gave us an eloquent answer to this conflict of cultural reciprocities. He talks about the American influences on the allegedly mainstream European culture. In his view, operating from a peripheral position not only implies a degree of filter, but also a degree of interpretation, the necessary reconstruction of the original source.

> Are there any specific experiences or biographical moments that shaped the way you think about architecture?

Sofia: There are too many. Everything affects the way you think, even if you are not conscious about it. Perhaps the most relevant moment for what we do today is the fact that we do it together. We met by chance and we decided to live and work together. That is indeed an accidental epiphany. In fact, we both grew up in different countries and received different educations. Maybe the good thing about it is that we never had a very strong influence from anyone. We started with a total sense of freedom.

Pezo: We never had to kill our fathers! So everything came to us in a very natural and direct manner. Every book we read, and every building or exhibition we visited around the world is somehow foreign to us. We can access it to a certain extent, it may exist at an intense or deep level, but we always feel there is something else, something more we are missing out on. At the same time, we are also happy to know that we are experiencing that information without the inevitable corset of those who grew up among the sources. In the end we trust our impressions and our raw experience more, without the nuances of a historical approach.

Sofia: I guess it is a good choice to work in a place you feel comfortable in because you know its codes, while also knowing that many of them are the result of layers of translations. The moment you go back to the original, you start wondering about the validity of the translations, and also become aware that your own codes are somehow dislocated from your own place. In some ways, we handle codes that are similar to those of our European architect friends, but we definitely don't belong to that culture. So there is always a friction. There is a familiarity interwoven with estrangement; there is both proximity and detachment.

Pezo: We are even distant from that ancient past even in our own continent. The great legacy of the ancient American cultures extended down to the north of Chile. But that is a foreign region even for us. In our southern extreme, life was nomadic, and therefore extremely fragile and ephemeral. I believe that sense of emptiness and distance must be infiltrating our perceptions, our constant questioning about what we are doing.

Sofia: And apart from that cultural distance, there is an actual physical distance that allows us to gain some time, to be slow in what we do. That pace gives us the right, or a sort of illusion of privilege at least, that we can still be original without obeying any school, attitude, or trend.

Pezo: In that sense, to assume that you have a hidden desire to be original—it's not because you have a desire to make something new or original or shocking, but perhaps an implied aspiration to go back to the origins, to the beginning, to the initial, basic questions of architecture. Therefore, if we do not have a background of theories, we invent the scaffolds for the ideas we want to pursue.

PEZO VON ELLRICHSHAUSEN, BLUE PAVILION,
ROYAL ACADEMY OF ARTS, LONDON, UK, 2014.

Sofia: I believe that the very distance becomes a filter through which we are able to flatten almost everything. We then try to reorganize it in a way that it makes sense to us, or simply to forget it and start from somewhere else.

How does your pedagogical work relate to your practice?

Pezo: We normally state that we work both in art and architecture, and that our practice is simultaneously an academic and professional one. We do almost the same amount of work inside and outside the cloister, in the so-called real world. What fascinates us about academia is its immediacy. There we can rapidly test ideas even as we train ourselves to be clear about how to determine an internal set of rules to develop an architectural project. That is something we normally try to teach, or rather to share with our students. It is what we call an education based on obstructions. In other words, the deliberate proposition of a fake problem—or more than fake, perhaps an illogical or arbitrary problem—that has to be solved in a logical way. Thus, instead of trying to assume an artistic freedom within the academic realm, just because it is, by definition, deprived from the real constraints of the world, we are trying to develop the student's capacity to solve problems in an architectonic way. We believe that this is more useful for students to learn, instead of learning any sort of stylistic approach or technique. After all, that instructive knowledge can be found in many books. Instead, we are trying to train an intellectual capacity to solve specific problems with the tools of architecture. It is not about giving some formula for doing architecture but to train a deep understanding of the potential of developing a building.

Sofia: In academia, we try to narrow the discussion to a single subject, perhaps in opposition to the very simultaneity of the profession where you have to deal with many layers at once. These obstructions, sometimes we even call them traps, are really about focusing on a timely aspect of architecture. By doing so, we think we can dive deep into architectonic problems, and we can also develop our own position towards them.

Pezo: We agree that perhaps the only thing you can teach an architecture student is his or her capacity to solve problems. That is what we face every day as architects. In practice, there is a huge number of problems with many possible directions, from inserting a large surface into a small lot to working on a tiny budget, or any other limitation. Reality is full of constraints. But the directness to see problems, and to be able to start from the problems themselves is, in our view, at the core of any reasonable project.

What are your sources of inspiration or curiosities?

Sofia: We are very interested in art.

Pezo: We do art! We are not only interested in it.

Sofia: Yes, but for lateral references we look more at art than at architecture. In fact, for us, almost anything triggers our capacity to produce a building, or our capacity to react to a given problem. Perhaps not just to react, but also to put forward a certain position, sentence or statement. I think that anything that can somehow lead us in that direction, any work from the disciplinary or non-disciplinary world, is of interest to us.

Pezo: Mixing our art and architecture practices has enormous potential for us. It functions as a kind of double critique, a reciprocal evaluation from either side. And we try to see up to what point what we do has an artistic value in the field of architecture, or up to what point what we do as artists, a painting for example, might have an architectonic value. We are interested in exploring how we can translate those values from one field to the other. Or whether we can even assume that they both belong to the same field, and that everything coexists at the same level. Perhaps one of the issues that informs an artistic practice is an unapologetic sense of autonomy, a kind of self-referentiality to define its own set of values. It is indeed accepted that anything that an artist defines as a work of art is a work of art, period. It seems that nowadays, such arbitrariness, and capacity to validate the work by an internal set of references, is something that is difficult to defend in reference to a work of architecture. This is because today architecture tends to be over-justified by external conditions. Architects tend to explain a project according to the conditions of the site, the conditions of the budget, sustainability, urban problems, and so on. Yet we have lost the capacity to define, in a very logical manner, the elements that validate a work of architecture. Despite sounding rhetorical or even tautological, architecture is still a self-demarcated domain. The very disciplinary system tends to forget this foundational condition.

Sofia: It seems that we, practicing architects, have lost our intrinsic authority. It is not the diagrams or statistics that should empower us to have such a position. Of course, I know a great deal of reason is needed to solve a building, however, there is an over-rationalization of the practice. I guess there is nothing wrong with saying "this is not rational, but I am doing it regardless because I know where it is going."

> It appears as if you've disconnected the momentum of producing art from architecture. Is this correct?

PEZO VON ELLRICHSHAUSEN, CENT PAVILION,
CHICAGO ARCHITECTURE BIENNIAL,
CHICAGO, ILLINOIS, 2015. ELEVATION VIEW
FOREGROUNDED AGAINST CROWN HALL.

Sofia: We don't believe we can really disconnect one from the other. In fact, we do not label what we do into one or the other category. Distinctions are always problematic, and relative to what certain institutions want to read in them. Maybe the only distinction for us resides in the starting point for a project, which defines if it will be an art or an architectural work.

Pezo: The distinction is more an official one. A museum validates what a work of art is. But there are also academic or communication institutions. In practical terms, works are works.

Sofia: We never make an explicit distinction while working on a project. The only way of realizing your field of action is acknowledging if you are responding to external or internal demands. There is a conventional belief that an artwork starts before any circumstantial demand. It could be initiated by an impression, an intuition, an idea, or a statement, which then finds its way to be materialized.

> So you see art or architecture as something that starts when you have a question. I read that as kind of illogical, because you could also use architecture without a question from the client, for yourself, as art. Or do you only start to think about an architectural proposition when there is a client?

Sofia: That is a paradox. There are always some ideas in the air. The problem is how to turn them into a coherent piece of architecture. Sometimes the case implies a correspondence between circumstances and a priori intentions. Perhaps in art, you invent the circumstances in order to produce the case.

PEZO VON ELLRICHSHAUSEN, MERI HOUSE,
FLORIDA, CHILE, 2014.

Pezo: In many ways, this is something we have explored in our academic studios as well. The subtle distinction between arbitrariness and purpose, between what might be intentional or accidental. This is clearly related with the overlap between the fields of art and architecture. Following both the tradition of beaux arts or technical schools, we have been trained to say that architecture has to respond to a certain amount of evidence, to a certain amount of objective conditions, such as the code, the program, construction efficiency, and so on. Even prejudices about beauty. The articulation of those many factors should, therefore, result in a logical deduction, in a proper argument. Hence architecture appears as a mere consequence of those facts, as their synthetic outcome. This is definitely a reduction of the real scope of architecture. On the contrary, in art you can start and finish anywhere. The moment we assumed our practice navigates from one side to the other, we were voluntarily puzzling our own starting point.

Sofia: Maybe there is an artistic component in our architecture and an architectonic component in our art. This could be both at a level of intentions and also at a level of understanding of the final piece.

> Your exhibit, "Detached," at the 2010 Venice Architecture Biennale, talked directly about issues of architectural autonomy. How do you define autonomy in architecture, and how that could relate to these opportunities that come from the outside?

Sofia: More than autonomy, we were dealing with reciprocity. In that exhibition, we presented two different projects, or two different contexts: one being a house in a suburban setting, and the other a house in a remote, wild landscape. Each one has its own internal logic, or if you wish to say, autonomy—their own formal structure. The two cases were depicted through large backlit photographs, together with a free-standing small concrete scale model on a steel pedestal. With that clear opposition between object and background context, we were interested in up to what point our buildings are informed by or have an impact in their surroundings. We believe there is always a reciprocity. It is an endless dilemma to really know how much of what we do is actually able to impact what is around it. Its consequences somehow exceed the architect's expected supremacy.

Pezo: Perhaps there is even an ethical dimension associated to that capacity, or incapacity. By the very notion of "detachment" we were evaluating the strength of a building in terms of presence and character, up to the point of redefining the quality of its surroundings. As opposed to a European city, where you have to be humble out of sheer respect to history, most of our south American contexts are very fragile, unstable, and ever changing. Any new building almost implies doing something for the first time. Consequently, we believe that we must do something strong enough so as to amplify its impact. In other words, to concentrate intensity in order to produce more with less.

> If you're interested in radiating outward and affecting the context, is that a result of a political agenda, or some idea of resisting market forces?

Pezo: It may be no more than a survival instinct, a form of denial. After all, we operate under our own rules because we have not found something convincing to follow.

Sofia: In the case of the new suburbs, we have certainly reacted against its individualistic and pretentious nature, against the social conventions, the representational codes of a pointless and egoist form of life. Of course we feel compelled to resist those market forces, but to resist them while doing something else, something in exchange, without losing our deep faith in architecture.

PHYLLIS LAMBERT

As an IIT-educated architect who, prior to that, was the client for the Seagram Building, and later founded numerous policy-driven organizations and research-based cultural institutions, including Heritage Montréal and the Canadian Centre for Architecture (CCA) in Montréal, your life's work demonstrates the variety of roles an architect can inhabit to impact society that extend far beyond the scope of a designer. What are your thoughts on the unique potentials of architects that can be leveraged outside the field of architecture, whether it's in research, activism, politics, education, or any number of areas?

Lambert: I think first you have to start reflecting, as Mies [van der Rohe] did, on the state of the world: what kind of world are we living in, how can we improve that world or make the necessary changes, and stabilize aspects of it? There are different lenses through which you can approach these questions—politically, or through social justice; or in terms of the ways in which individuals relate to buildings and landscape, or through environmental concerns. In short, political ecology, social ecology, and scientific ecology. I think each person will find her or his role, outside or inside the field, but you need to be open to the wider view. The only way this can happen is if you think about architecture expansively enough.

Through your involvement in multiple organizations and the establishment of others, you've shown that active involvement in politics may be required to have an impact on the city. For example, the Institute of Political Alternatives of Montréal (IPAM), which you founded and are actively engaged in, is a citizens' initiative whose mission is to contribute to viable urban planning, economic and sustainable development, and local democracy in Montréal. How effective has IPAM been in achieving these goals?

Lambert: IPAM moved—and continues to move—very quickly. We organized the first public consultation on territorial planning for the Montréal Metropolitan Community, which set the stage for annual public assessment. Today, we hold roundtables for problems of immediate concern, such as the repurposing of the large, abandoned hospitals that have been replaced by new ones, and discuss our findings with members of the city administration. And we're going to have a meeting on what's next, because we have a new mayor now. There was no vision before for the city, in terms of priorities for planning, housing, transportation, or the many issues of city and suburb. It was all rather narrow: people were looking at aspects of removing snow from the streets, or fixing potholes. You have to look at something far larger than that, such as what greater Montréal will look like in the future; that's a problem of the suburbs as well as the central city.

I have also been involved for many years in not-for-profit social housing renovation in difficult areas of the city, often where people with very little money, mainly immigrants, settle. We cannot allow cities to be increasingly for the rich, and so we invest in the second mortgage to improve multi-residential buildings, simply by repointing the exterior, replacing windows and doors, painting them inside, and replacing the plumbing and electricity. The buildings are not of any architectural value, but access to healthy, livable residential units should be the right of all citizens, and upgrading deeply affects the lives of families in areas where there is crime, and children are growing up with difficulties. We try to do it in areas that have at least some social infrastructure in place to eliminate crime, so that it offers hope to children and new families.

> Is that what you've been doing with Fonds d'Investissement de Montreal (FIM)? Has that been an economically viable model?

Lambert: Yes, we get better returns on our investment than the banks do! It's a terrific program.

> How have you been able to make it so successful?

Lambert: FIM is a limited partnership. Its small board of directors consists of people with experience in renovation, social housing, and real-estate law. We were able to convince corporations, companies, and foundations to invest as limited partners. The investors in FIM include the union-collective, Fonds de solidarité des travailleurs du Québec (FTQ), and an association of credit unions, the Fédération des Caisses Desjardins, which are the major investors, as well the public utility, Hydro-Québec, the Banque Nationale, and others, including some foundations.

The rules governing foundations have changed, allowing them to invest in not-for-profit organizations. One foundation involved with us is able to double the investment of others. It is interested in low income families, particularly children, so they request that we have projects on hand with at least two, preferably three or four, bedrooms, and we try to accommodate that. Each FIM has invested about $5 million each time, and we are enormously pleased that our fourth

FIM raised four times that amount after we approached more potential investors.

The program's success rests on the perception that there is a serious need for affordable housing beyond what governments feel that they can invest. Furthermore, the FIM's management is very light, thanks to Technical Resource Groups (GRT), who take on all aspects of identifying and financing projects, and work with local organizations. So the GRT finds houses for us and we, the board, say "yay" or "nay," or discuss whatever other issues we think need to be addressed; the investors have the final word. We always work with fairly large projects: the first three phases of FIM assured that over a 1,000 families had access to decent homes at affordable prices.

It seems like a relatively open discussion.
Lambert: Yes, we ask the investors if they approve, and if they do, we go ahead and arrange a second mortgage for the project.

Is that now accepted as a possible model?
Lambert: We took the basic model from the United States, we didn't invent it ourselves. It's the only one in Canada, I think. Of course, each jurisdiction has its own modalities. I love it, and I think it's a great project, as well as a great investment on the part of corporations in the well-being of families, and thus of the city.

It seems that you are an advocate for a bottom-up approach to achieve a more democratic city, and incorporate social needs. Is the contemporary metropolis lacking in this mode of activism, and does that in turn lead to difficulty in maintaining socio-economic diversity?

Lambert: Yes, absolutely. One of the things that has worked wonderfully in planning and developing new projects in Montréal—which I think should happen everywhere—is to have local input for everything. This works on two levels: first, overall input to the city through citizens' organizations such as IPAM and Héritage Montréal, and input at public consultation for projects. We successfully initiated the practice of public consultation when a commercial developer wanted to privatize a public street in downtown Montréal—and this with the support of the then-mayor! That project was stopped. Subsequently, public consultation became a major tool in convincing the federal government to maintain the Vieux Port, the old port of Montréal, as a public good. Someone had had the bright idea to bring in a firm such as Gerald D. Hines to develop commercial structures on the quays, and an internationally recognized architect made a proposal to build "London-type" residential squares at the edge of the river in front of the authentic architecture of the seventeenth to nineteenth century historical city that had grown there, which made no sense at all on so many levels. So we had public hearings and people said, no, the land should be there for the people of Montréal to use and enjoy, simply by maintaining and reusing the great industrial warehouses on the quays for public purposes. Initially, public consultation was not part of the city's charter, and the next mayor came in and wiped it out. We then made sure that public consultation was enshrined in the charter. To give you a sense of the bottom-up nature of activism, we have various citizen advisory councils in neighborhoods that are essential for sane development, the most significant of which is the Table de Concertation, a consulting round table that advises on what the neighborhood perceives as needed. For example, they raise money to commission studies on strengths and weak-

PHYLLIS LAMBERT AND MILTON-PARC CITIZENS,
MONTRÉAL, CANADA, JANUARY 21, 1983.

nesses, map them, and then discuss these reports with the city. It's the people in the neighborhoods, and the people throughout the city who live with problems, that should be heard. A huge amount of intelligence, knowledge and creativity resides in the population, so why is all the control handed to a couple of bureaucrats?

> So you're leading coordination between different parties to create a voice for the people with needs?

Lambert: Well, it's not just about people with needs, it is about the concept of the city. There are a whole lot of municipalities in Montréal, and only some of the counselors are sympathetic to public input. So you try to let people know how impressive and useful this form of planning is. There are also a number of small groups that talk to the mayor about the issues at stake, like IPAM, as well as the usual lobbies. The more people with whom you interact or bring into your tent, the better it is for architecture. My experience has been that public consultation has had a very positive effect on projects, and those areas of the city in which there has been no public input, such as Griffintown in Montréal, are very disappointing, socially and architecturally.

> You've been a strong advocate for architectural preservation. Before selling the Seagram Building, you pushed for its complete preservation. On another occasion, you were displeased with changes made to the Segal Centre for the Performing Arts [formerly Saidye Bronfman Centre]. What criteria do you use to judge a building's quality to argue that it is worth preserving?

Lambert: Sometimes it is clear. The Seagram Building was a major work from the very beginning. This has to be

the opinion of many others—that the building is meaningful to them, architecturally, socially, historically, or
maybe only as an element giving identity to a neighborhood. In Quebec there are very good preservation laws
and so you would, for example, make a presentation
on the value of a park or a building, and it must gain
government approval to be listed and therefore be pro-
tected. It's always a process, which can be very complicated; for example, zoning changes to increase density
can make protecting a building unviable. You don't just
get to say this is a great building. You have to prove it,
and persuade others why it contributes to the neighborhood, and to the society it's embedded in.

If we are continually preserving buildings and
repurposing them, do you see space for new
architecture in the metropolis?

Lambert: Plenty of it. Old industrial or military reserve
areas, or spaces made obsolete by other technological
change, such as post offices. Think of the Hudson Yards
in New York City and the long abandoned Michael Reese
Hospital site in Chicago. But they must be planned according to needs. In Montréal, a manufacturer of planes
and trains and such obviously looked down one day from
his pinnacle in the business district and saw this fairly
flat site in an old industrial area, and funded some sec-
ond-rate suburban builder/developer who went to the
city and said, "Okay, we can do something." That something competed at first with the functions of other areas
in the city, and finally ended up being filled with condo-
miniums. So people protested it, and after construction
of 60 percent of the site, the city held public hearings.
Not every building in an area like that that needs to stay,
and there are empty lots too. But, it's a question of studying the whole area and what the issues are. There's always
plenty of room in cities for new construction.

We had an interesting discussion during the public hearings on landmark status for the Seagram Building in 1980. One person pointed out that Park Avenue had been zoned in 1916 so that all the buildings were residential and the same height. In 1930, landowners in the area decided that they would make much more money if the area below 57th Street were zoned commercial. So it was re-zoned and nobody cared at the time with the Wall Street crash focusing their attention and the Great Depression setting in. But after the Second World War, that 1930s zoning kicked in, and the area changed quite dramatically. It became a rare area in New York City with ambitious architecture.

> Through these projects you try to increase awareness of the role of architecture in contemporary society. The CCA is based on the premise that "architecture is a public concern," which it addresses in publications and exhibitions, and through research and scholarship in the field. Why is public awareness so important for you?

Lambert: If you don't have a public that wants something better, politicians are not going to move. They listen to the voices of the people who are going to elect them, and they don't take time to do the studies we do. It's up to the citizens to say we can make this a great city. Occasionally, you get a mayor like Mayor Drapeau, who changed Montréal enormously for the better, bringing it into the mid-twentieth century. Unfortunately, when he did so he also destroyed whole areas that really didn't have to be demolished—public input just did not exist then. But typically there is just inaction, and you need people who are aware of how the city works—not just one building, but how whole areas fit into the rest of the city—and know how to instigate. For example, the

Quartier International de Montreal (QIM) is an area that traverses an open cut in the fabric of the city. That cut was made in the 1960s for the East-West [Ville-Marie] expressway, back when everything was designed for cars. In a strong gesture, the QIM project covered the expressway, and created two new landscaped public spaces, without any demolition required. The sophisticated Édifice Jacques-Parizeau, designed as the headquarters for the Caisse de dépôt et de placement du Québec, a para-governmental financial institution, surrounds an exciting indoor atrium, forming a third public space. Facing it is the extension to the 1960s convention hall [the Palais des congrès de Montréal], so you've got about three-quarters of a mile of planned new development. It's rare to find architects who make good use of the material on hand. The project was proposed and designed by a young woman, architect and urban designer Renée Daoust, of Daoust Lestage. The president of the Caisse made sure that everyone in the surrounding area was in agreement from the start. Formerly a desolate area in the city, within a few years the QIM stimulated billions of dollars of investment in good quality buildings, and the area was transformed. Those are the kinds of exciting things that can happen in the city if you have public and private groups working together. There was an awful lot of brain power and energy invested for free in all of this. This is one of the great things that we can do as architects.

Getting back to the Seagram Building for a moment, the Seagram was economically viable and architecturally powerful, and valued social relevance over iconicity. What sort of approach or mindset is needed today to achieve a project of a similar quality to the Seagram?

Lambert: It has to be a commitment to the city. If you're

going to build a building, you have to have a commitment to more than just yourself; you must have a commitment to people who live in it, to people who live
around it, to a much wider area than your site. You're
making an intervention in the city, and everybody should
keep that in mind when commissioning and designing a
new building.

> Since its inception, the Seagram Building has
> become one of the most copied buildings in
> the world. In a majority of cases, the Seagram
> is copied in its image but not in its ideas,
> which were much more powerful. Dedicating
> a large space in front of the building as a pub-
> lic plaza, for example, not only demonstrated
> generosity and respect for the architecture of
> the city, but it also influenced New York City's
> zoning code, which subsequently created in-
> centivized zoning. In the metropolis of today,
> do you believe that the Seagram Building is
> still a valid precedent for new buildings in in-
> creasingly dense cities?

Lambert: Yes, by setting the building back and creating a public space in New York City, Seagram changed
the zoning code so that developers could get, for one
square-foot of open space, ten square feet of added volume to the building. So everybody did it, which changed
the city very much. But there was a problem, because
the legislation that put this into place didn't say very
much about what the quality of those spaces should be.
William H. Whyte, who wrote The Organization Man,
said to the city, look, you're not getting value for your
dollar—look at all those empty concrete spaces with no
amenities. So the city started to change the legislation
and require a sculpture or other amenities and places
for people to sit, and so on. I think the first gesture is

MIES VAN DER ROHE, SEAGRAM BUILDING, NEW
YORK CITY, NEW YORK, 1957.

great, but then you have to monitor and keep improving on that gesture.

> The visual arts played a major role in the curriculum of the Bauhaus and IIT. A number of Miesian buildings also feature sculptures and public amenities to balance the rigidity of the modular grid and energize the space. There's no question that public art, like The Flamingo at the Federal Center, can contribute to a contemporary city, but they aren't always successful. If you were to position a work of art in the context of the Seagram Building, what would be your criteria for its success?

Lambert: That's very easy to say. Much of the art and design of the plazas that zoning change ensured was weak. It has to be well thought out, and you need to have advisers whose work and thought is concerned with the role of art in the city. At the Seagram building for example, we said that any sculpture—any work or object—that goes on the plaza needed to be approved by MoMA.

> In your lifetime, you've had the opportunity to experience Mies's architectural pedagogy as both a client and as a student of Mies. What aspects of Mies's original curriculum at IIT do you feel are still applicable and important to maintain in today's context of "Rethinking the Metropolis"?

Lambert: I think that his curriculum, or rather his idea of, first of all, be careful what you do, keep your pencil sharp and your paper clean, is a good thing to know, and also to work logically, to work with the materials, to understand materials. He said, "Architecture starts when you put two bricks together." That's a marvelous place to start because a brick is something you can just hold in your hand, and then put another one in your hand. There's no technological ordeal you have to go through to do that. Of course it becomes more complicated after that, but it is grounding. It's grounding of how and what you need to learn. Mies was also very interested in urban or city planning and you learned about that in much the same way as how to layout a kitchen—for example, what you do with the dishes when you put them on the left side or the right side of the sink. These are simple, wonderful things. The primary things, I think that's where you ought to start.

> Since its founding, the CCA has successfully established itself as a center for architectural research, exhibitions, lectures, and films. What unique aspects of the CCA do you think have allowed it to succeed as a platform for architectural discussion?

Lambert: At the CCA, it is not about looking at architecture as an object, rather it's about looking at the environment in which architecture exists. If you look at the exhibitions that we've had, one was the "Sense of the City" in 2005; we are always highlighting the visual aspects of cities, but there are also smells, sounds, the seasons of the year, and so on. These factors affect the city very much. Another exhibition and publication, "Imperfect Health: The Medicalization of Architecture" in 2011, uncovers some of the uncertainties and contradictions in the current idea of health and considers how architecture acknowledges, incorporates, and affects health issues and cultural conceptions of health. With "The Archaeology of the Digital," we were really pioneers in working with the specificity of born digital material in the way that it is created, disseminated, and experienced. "1973: Sorry, Out of Gas" looked at energy-conserving architecture; architects were experimenting in that area as early as the 1930s. So we've been looking at issues emanating from building, but not the building itself necessarily. The CCA asks people to think. It asks questions that usually aren't asked. In that respect the discourse is highly intelligent.

> Rem Koolhaas once said that since Philip Johnson appeared on the cover of Time magazine in 1979, architects may have gained prominence, but they lost social relevance. What do you think has changed?

Lambert: Peter Eisenman and I hated the book, *Philip Johnson: Life and Work*, by your local historian, [Franz] Schulze. We were very unhappy for Philip; emphasis on his sexual life colors the work, overlooking how Philip was a real patron for architecture. So we organized a conference [Autonomy and Ideology: Positioning an Avant-Garde in America, 1996] on the state of the avant-garde today, and one of the things we learned was that when Philip curated the 1932 exhibition on the International style, none of the social aspects that were central in Europe were mentioned in it. It was just not part of the American tradition. The Museum of Modern Art (MoMA) recently did an exhibition investigating solutions to social housing in the United States [Foreclosed: Rehousing the American Dream, 2011], but I don't think the solutions proposed dealt with core issues. The problems are hugely challenging, and we don't know how to build social housing. I think it's... American values—idolizing the rich, reviling the poor. By the way, on the Time magazine cover, Philip was holding the model of his AT&T building with that silly top on it. He had the temerity to say he thought AT&T was up there with the Seagram Building. He was expressing the values of the day. So I think that Rem was really criticizing all of society, not necessarily just Philip.

The CCA has also functioned as a forum for architectural debate. What do you consider to be the most important discourse that we, as architects, should be having today?

Lambert: It's the discourse on the city, and how the social, ecological, transport, and landscape components can come together. It's looking at the things we don't consider. You have to be able to hear the birds; you have to be able to smell the flowers. These make for a very interesting, humane way of looking at the city.

So you have an ecological take on the city as a system in which various species can develop.

Lambert: Yes, that's what we are, aren't we? A species?

Bruno Latour, the French sociologist, once said that our future might depend on the way in which we choose to handle relations between humans and non-humans. He would say non-humans include computers, robots, and other inventions by humans, as well as dogs and animals.

Lambert: It's because we've changed. If you think of [The Epic of] Gilgamesh from 2000 BC it was, everything was so utterly physical and sensual—it was just great. We've left these things behind, so the question is how do we re-integrate the direct and the sensible into our lives, together with the wonderful new tools we've invented?

Would you say that these tools are innocent or that they imply a certain level of performance, organization, and different ways to think, for example, a pencil versus the computer? At the Barrage in the United States, we would have all these debates with [Kenneth] Frampton that paralleled the paperless studio in Columbia and what Greg Lynn is now organizing on digital archaeology. We would debate with Frampton who would say, "do you really believe that Bill Gates is putting out innocent products on a mass scale?" Some people believed it was simply a tool. Others would argue no, these tools do imply certain social relationships.

Lambert: But it's we who make them do things, they don't do it on their own. It's because we wanted them to do that. It's like our religions and our laws. We make those things for ourselves.

In the near future, in twenty or thirty years, we may have a computer, or an apparatus, or robot, that will not only be able to think in a very logical way, but maybe it can also have a combinatorial possibility that will allow it to develop and become creative. It could be that we produce something that is capable of reproducing itself.

Lambert: Yes of course it's speculation but maybe people who are really into what computers can do, more than my simplistic knowledge of it, can offer more complicated visions. It's still, off, on, off on, 1, 0, 1, 0. If you go back to philosophy, where the usual question was, "is man born innocent?" or "is he a war animal?" what do you do about that? We can make as many abstract or artificial processes as we want but how do we make a more decent world? What do you think?

When we talk about architecture nowadays it's about museums, performance spaces, and icons, whereas in the 1920s and 1930s when Mies was dealing with the Weissenhofsiedlung, it was about the social; in the whole of

SAMUEL BRONFMAN COMMENDING PHYLLIS
LAMBERT ON THE FIRST DAY HE OCCUPIED
HIS OFFICE IN THE SEAGRAM BUILDING,
DECEMBER 23, 1957.

Europe, the issue of the social was very important. In 1902, when the housing law was passed giving everyone the right to social housing in the Netherlands [Housing Act of 1902], architects were heavily involved. The Berlage Institute in Amsterdam South had a huge urban development which remains very important to this day, and is one of the most interesting housing/urban planning projects in Europe. So, what is the relevance of the architectural debate at this moment on these social issues?

Lambert: I think that's where the discussion should be rather than the marvelous planet we are going to have where the computers are running everything. Again, it's the things like the management of trees or water... look at the little pond that was made by Jeanne Gang up by the [Lincoln Park] Zoo, which uses run-off water instead of fresh water. There are so many little things that can be done just to make ecological, humane, and palpable improvements. People say, well, you're not going to solve the problem just by using less energy and composting. Individually perhaps not, but eventually collectively. I think that that's where the issue lies. How many people in this world are living miserably? Humanitarians always say we have to save the lives of the newborn, but they never say, if we save these children's lives in severely resource-limited communities, what kind of life are they going to live? These are the questions that need to be asked. Of course we love technical things. Look at medicine, it's brilliant, but it's all technical.

But medicine is also like water or food in a way, because without water, food, and oxygen, you die. So there's deprivation on the one hand, and on the other hand we try to make our lives longer and better, now living to a hundred-plus from an average age of fifty only fifty years ago.

Lambert: It changes society.

Yes, the rise in the number of older people has been dramatic. In Japan, for example, the people that are sixty-five and up probably comprise 50 percent of the population. It's about how we handle that and deal with the issues that arise. When we talk about Nowness as our approach at this school, what we're saying is that you have to identify the issues of the moment, and how we can contribute. When we look at the topic of "Building Seagram," it's a great example of how a city has to deal with the public realm; the area around and even inside the building is dealing with this public realm. The public realm is of course extremely important for what we do in Chicago, and in the world, and I think that's also why you're interested. I'm very happy that IIT students are having this debate with you about social issues, about activist issues. I think architects in the twentieth century were radical activists, and in Russia they were thinking about the new revolutionary society.

Lambert: In Germany too.

And Germany, the Netherlands, Italy, and so on. So what is the position of American students on social issues? Do you have the courage to make a manifesto, not only to talk about the icon, but rather to talk about society and how it has to change?

Lambert: I remember the first young people that started to make in-roads into life were The Beatles. All of a sudden our generation could do something. And look at the people working with technology who are making the changes today: your kids are way ahead of you, and everyone younger is way ahead of them, not only in technology, but regarding environmental and moral issues. So it's fascinating to think about where they will go.

> That's also bottom-up. The younger people making a difference aren't the people established in different positions.

Lambert: We could say something similar about the role of women. Women as architects have, in the last generation, become a very strong force and that has become manifest in the young today who are responsible for decisions tomorrow.

> India just launched a space program for Mars. So it's Europe, America, Russia, and India. On the other hand, there are hundreds of millions of people in India that are living below the poverty line. So, let us find both strategies to go to Mars, but also a strategy for the conditions in which people are living.

Lambert: I remember going to the Museum of Science in Florence some years ago [now the Museo Galileo] which displayed beautiful fruit-wood planes on which to roll a ball down, and exquisitely etched brass sextants, and such. Then there was a medical area, which showed instruments like ghastly iron forceps used in child-birth, and all sorts of horrible looking saws to cut bones with. I thought, goodness, the human being didn't count. The beautiful, sophisticated things were created for scientific use and research. We still have the same problem.

I agree, I also think there are many fields that you can learn from, including medicine, music, cinema, or philosophy. I believe in educating yourself. But architecture has a discipline and it's very important that you know your field. Part of the question is whether you will continue working as an architect your entire life. You are perhaps trained as an architect at this institute, but maybe you will change in a couple of years.

Lambert: Look at the practice of Diller Scofidio + Renfro. They're astounding. I think they were able to do the Lincoln Center commission, fraught with every problem you can think, because they had investigated creative conceptual ideas making films and exhibitions. But because of that, they had the openness of mind and the ability to not only solve problems but to develop new ways of solving them. They came in and did not say they want to change the Lincoln Center, but rather to make it more than it is.

Yes, you do not necessarily need to have a lot of experience to make a big impact.

Lambert: I talked about that in my book. Kahn and Jacobs were the associate architects of the Seagram Building. They had recently become "modern" with stripy [Erich] Mendelsohn-style buildings in New York City—facades of ribbon windows rather than punched holes. They were touted as the most competent architects of postwar buildings in New York City. So when Eli Jacques Kahn came to Mies's office in New York City—I had my office there too—he had the attitude that Mies was a child, doing these simple buildings and told him quite patronizingly, you know, New York City is very complex, quite complicated. Kahn said, "I tell you how we do it, Mies. We start with a ground plan and then we work the elevator core, and in this building it would be about so many elevators, to do the job quickly. And then we start decorating the door like this..." And Mies just said, "No, that is not what I do!" So that's the story of Seagram.

POWER
RIKEN YAMAMOTO

You were a graduate student at the time of the Osaka International Exposition in 1970. What impact, if any, did it have on you as a young architect starting your professional career?

Yamamoto: It had a strong impact. I was just twenty-five when I visited the Osaka Exposition. I was seriously disappointed by the American pavilion with "air" inside. Not symbolic air, but actually just air. There was a long queue of people waiting to enter this pavilion because the Americans had recently gone to the moon, and they had brought back this small moonstone. The "architecture" at the pavilion consisted of only the air and the stone. I thought the architecture at the rest of the pavilions was not that good. I do remember the pavilion for Czechoslovakia though. They had a live performance with people and a number of screens that projected images. As the actors moved, the screens moved with them, even to the outside. The images changed rapidly, and the actors and the images worked together as a performance. That had a strong impact on me, although, again, there was no actual architecture; instead the image was more important in creating space and movement.

Did you consider it to be contemporary architecture?

Yamamoto: Yes, that was contemporary to me. Even the actors and actresses were anonymous, and less significant than the image. I begin to question the possibility of realizing the image as actual architecture in the future. At the time, however, I still thought vernacular architectures were better. So when I graduated school, I went to work for Hiroshi Hara. He had studied various examples of village communities, and we began traveling all over the world. I was one of the first Japanese students that had gone outside the country to study vernacular architecture. Modern architecture was very popular with Japanese architects, and at that moment there was no interest in vernacular architecture of other countries. So we travelled. Kengo Kuma also travelled, but he went to Africa with Mr. Hara.

Did you visit Chicago and Crown Hall during your time abroad?

Yamamoto: I visited many countries, but it was vernacular architecture that I was deeply interested in at that moment. I did visit Chicago a long time ago in the 1980s, when I was a lecturer. That was my first time in America, and Chicago made a huge impact on me compared to New York City. The cityscape in Chicago is very different from other American cities. After the fire, the city changed. Wacker drive was built, with lower and upper levels. I was interested also in Frank Lloyd Wright and [Louis] Sullivan. I was amazed with Sullivan's Auditorium Building. This building was more powerful to me than modern architecture because it was in between the modern and nineteenth century architecture.

Sullivan was proto-modern, like [Hendrik] Berlage.

Yamamoto: Sullivan's architecture was something like a spectacle. The interior of the Auditorium Building made a strong impression on me. But there were always two ways to do modernism: Sullivan and Mies van der Rohe. I did visit Mies's National Museum in Berlin, but Chicago was the first city where I had experienced such a rigid Miesian site plan, namely IIT where all of the buildings are very rigid, square and simple. Here in S. R. Crown Hall, I had my first experience of the modern building. At that moment I preferred Chicago to any other city, and that was the reason I wanted to come again. I was excited to come again for the cityscape. Chicago leaves an even better impression now because it is very green and beautiful. I made a book titled *The Power of Space and the Space of Power* [2015]—in Japanese—to explain the origins of modernism as I understood them; it had discussions ranging from the Deutscher Werkbund movement to Sachlichkeit, and elaborates on the impact these early movements had on modernism.

> I believe your book also references Hannah Arendt?

Yamamoto: Hannah Arendt has given another kind of meaning to modernism, and this book presents a slight contradiction of her idea. It agrees with her, but not entirely. I found it a little difficult to say that the idea of modernism was comparable to the idea of Nazism, as she did. She compared them through their similarities, and it was clear that she did not agree with modernism.

> Arendt proposed the "vita activa," or active life. She did not agree with functionalism because modernist structures are too rigid.

Yamamoto: Yes, she also said that functionalism was a big problem because functionalism was made only from necessity. She believed that our own thoughts were more important than necessity, which is a contradiction in my mind. It is important that we now rethink the meaning of modernism again. My theory, which I published in my book, is inspired by the theory of Hannah Arendt. For her, the city is a political space. Consider this excerpt from *The Human Condition* [University of Chicago Press, 1958]: "Not the interior of this private realm,

RIKEN YAMAMOTO, SEOUL GANGAM HOUSING,
SEOUL, KOREA, 2014.

which remains hidden and of no public significance, but its exterior appearance is important for the city as well, and it appears in the realm of the city through the boundaries between one household and the other. The law originally was identified with this boundary line, which in ancient times was still actually a space, a kind of no–man's–land between the private and the public." According to Arendt, what we normally think of as a boundary is actually a space. The meeting between houses was a space, called no–man's–land. I was perplexed by this at first because no–man's–land translates to a space for no people, in Japanese. But in the western understanding, it is when the space between two spaces is "sheltering and protecting both realms while, at the same time, separating them from each other." So no–man's–land is a very important term, and I use a very similar concept in my ideas and research.

> Could you elaborate on how you have tried to rethink modernism?

Yamamoto: My reference goes back to antiquity and Hippodamus's town plan for Miletus, which is based on the grid. It was the plan of equality and a rational social order. Within this grid, each house is connected to the public realm by the street that adjoins the two distinct spaces. This imposes a very political idea on the public and private realms in the colony. Many colonial cities were built on this principle. The colonizers imposed a grid plan that implied certain rules, or a system of governance. In this historical context, boundaries can be equated to the law, so that when someone respected a set of boundaries, they were also following the law.

There is a clear threshold between the public and private realms. The character of the private realm is different from our understanding of the Oikos: a public space within a private dwelling is called Andron, and the lower part is called Oikia. Together, the Andron and Oikia forms an unit called Oikos. Women and slaves were not allowed in the Andron, because it was the space meant for men to eat, drink, and discuss freely. Therefore the word is a masculine term. Inversely, the Oikia is seen as the private space in the house—the "women's space"—and is a feminine noun. We typically understand this differentiation as two different intensities of privacy. However, the original definition of privacy implied isolation from the spaces where you had the freedom to participate in political life.

I think that we define the ancient Greek polis by its freedom and glory, but it is precisely the threshold between public and private realms that guarantees the freedom to have political discussions. Our houses nowadays are much like the Oikia in the Greek house—we have lost the place to participate in politics within the boundaries of our homes. According to Arendt, having that threshold for freedom is a political phenomenon connected to the rise of big city-states, which were embodiments of a philosophy regarding freedom for the polity that was manifested in the ancient city grid. The cities were put together as a political organization under the condition of certain rules regarded as law. There is no division between the rulers and the ruled, both parties are considered equal under the rules of the law. We now think of this as isonomia. Therefore, architecture and city planning are increasingly seen as original and even philosophical ideas. The grid plan and thresholds between public and private are examples that illustrate the importance to guarantee the freedom to participate in political discourse.

> Wouldn't you agree that contemporary architecture has often guaranteed a lack of freedom as well?

Yamamoto: The Crystal Palace was presented at the 1851 London exposition, and became immensely popular. At the same time, Prince Albert presented a model for cottages that served as laborer homes. The authorities were afraid that a similar situation to the 1848 February Revolution of Paris, or the March Revolution in Berlin, would create chaos in London, so an urban plan that isolated houses from each other was implemented. This idea was also demonstrated in Ludwig Hilberseimer's High Rise City project in 1924. Every house was allocated two or three windows, and all the houses were similar. This was what he called civilization. This policy of standardization permeated through twentieth century modernism and it is still realized in some cities today. The private sphere had no windows, no "no-man's-land," and especially lacked a relation to the outside. It's a space ruled by bureaucracy: private space was lost to the government.

What is your understanding of the city today? Yamamoto: We are now living in such a city where the elements of the polis that ensured freedom and equality have disappeared. The way we live now is an isolated condition; it is as though we are outside of the city, even outside the house. We are living to the typical "one house, one family system" that dominated the twentieth century. Moreover, houses are isolated from each other. There is no relationship between neighbors, and there is a complete absence of community. Even within the family, chores and tasks have become independent of one another. Housework mandates the policy and maintenance of a household; it introduces the place to the people living there. So, it is critical that we devise a different format of living from the "one house, one family system." It is difficult, because it is such an entrenched norm in the modernized world. Regardless of size, America and Japan are both experiencing the difficulties of isolation and lack of community in this system. I think we should think of different ideas of living.

> How have you advanced new ideas of collective living in your own work?

Yamamoto: I completed a project on the "one house, one family" situation with students at the Yokohama National University, in collaboration with companies such as Nissan Motors and Tokyo Gas Company. Back in 1960, the population in Tokyo was around ten people per household, but today it has changed drastically to 1.98 persons per household—that is less than two people! This number demonstrates that many of us live alone, which is particularly hard on Japan's aging population where 24.7 percent are elderly.

We proposed a community area for 500 people. The distribution consisted of 27 percent for those over sixty-five years old, 11 percent for children, and 60 percent for working adults. The system rested on a divided unit for two people, with a small private room and one sleeping space. The opening to the outside uses two shops for the threshold condition. In some areas they would come together to make a bigger shop in the middle. The bedroom is very small, as it was the living quarters and the park that would make up one house. The threshold spaces can serve a variety of programmatic organizations, such as the park, the bookshop, an atelier, and others. When combined, a basic loop is formed between five to seven houses with mini-kitchens and bathrooms. This would mean that the threshold space can act as a free market, where people lead collective lives. The units provided a basic continuity, with potentials to create a more vigorous loop. There are small, medium, and an extra-large loops. The larger loops have the capacity for 500 people, with programs such as a big restaurant, kitchen, spa, laundry, rental locker, or co-generation unit. There is also professional support for the employment of the global community within the circle system. They can participate in the care of the elderly, in the nursery, the convenience store, the consultant desk, and so on. The environment is designed such that there is a constant exchange of service and help.

What are the infrastructural needs of such a project?

Yamamoto: The transportation infrastructure is designed to have three to four lanes, which makes access to the houses and shops much easier by incorporating electric cars. I have had many difficulties trying to realize this proposal, and some municipalities I met with refused this idea, saying that they think it is impossible, because it is so different from the "one house, one family" system that they have grown accustomed to.

Were you able to see this prototype become a thriving community?

Yamamoto: It was not built in Japan, but one instance of similar architectural experimentation that did get built was in Pangyo, Korea, in 2010. The proposal had a hundred houses on three stories. The lower level is a living room, the middle is the entrance, and the upper level is the bedroom. There is a common deck with a large entrance space, which manifested from the idea of the threshold. The living room is below the parking space. The hundred dwelling units are divided into groups of nine, eleven, or twelve houses. If you look at the section, it displays the relationship between the common deck, access, and the bedrooms. Walls are made of a transparent material, and people can use and customize the common deck freely by putting flowers or furniture where they please. The house and terrace space can also be customized; the terrace is sometimes used as a coffee shop. The transparency is not a problem because the level of privacy is adjusted, especially in the threshold space.

> In several of your projects, you use local traditions to form completely new conditions of living. Is this a response to social needs for new typologies, or is it a form of resistance to globalization?

Yamamoto: Both. I recognized that to address the isolation created by the "one house, one family" system, which is reaching a global scale due to investor and governmental demands, a new typology is required to resolve the lack of communal relationships between households. It is mandatory to reestablish a local community that works and lives together.

> Is hybrid programming perhaps a way to achieve social change?

Yamamoto: I believe so. The local community system creates an environment that allows different programs to coexist with one another. The integration of working and living provides a sense of responsibility. In other words, the people within the local community are contributing directly to make changes based on their day-to-day lives. This is the meaning of hybrid programming.

> Do you think architecture is capable of establishing new social patterns by itself, and if not, how can it act effectively to swerve already established social patterns?

Yamamoto: Social patterns are embedded in the typology of housing. We design housing and we should try to make use of that opportunity to make changes. The Shinonome Canal Court [2005] is a project that aims to establish new social patterns by itself. A standard building in Shinonome is fourteen stories high; the maximum height is only forty-seven meters but the density in that neighborhood is in the thousands. I think a better way is to limit buildings to within ten stories, like in the old Chicago. We should propose it instead of building high-rises. Shinonome does not function as a "one house, one family" system, but as a Small Offices / Home Offices unit mixture. The mixture means that we do not only have private housing but also home-business units. The hybrid program of home-business will become very important in the future. We should make a housing system that not only retains privacy, but will create a community, and a viable economic situation within housing. Many twentieth century architects had similar ideas on how to live and work together. Now we should propose more models with similar typology.

How do the users react to your diverse, transparent spaces that blur the division between private and public?

Yamamoto: I have often proposed living rooms that face each other to create a good communal space. You may think such communal ideas are the norm, but it is not so obvious for many. The dwellers have expressed to me that the spaces are easy to use, but I sometimes struggle with the municipality. They are very afraid to lose privacy, so they refuse to make their buildings transparent. Recently, I lost a job because of it. In a few cases, I designed entrances with a face-to-face situation against municipality rules, which they weren't happy about. The problem with their idea of privacy is that it limits access, which contradicts their mission as a public building. The idea of protecting the privacy of each unit above all else is a hangover from the twentieth century. Today, privacy is maximized in Japan's housing even as there is a lack of access and communal space; it's the same in high-rises

RIKEN YAMAMOTO, SEOUL GANGAM HOUSING,
SEOUL, KOREA, 2014. TOWERS AND FOUR-STORY
HOUSING WITH COMMUNAL ROOF GARDENS.

too, even though it is easy to retain privacy when only one person lives inside. It is done this way for security reasons.

The Circle at Zurich Airport is a unique project that blurs the generic reading of inside versus outside, resulting in a hybrid system of public space. How did you come to this approach?

Yamamoto: There was a moment in the competition where the judges said that this was not a supermarket but a city. The project was criticized as being between architecture, the city, and the town. My vision was to make The Circle a small downtown. Zürich is a charming city in the mountains, and the terrain is quite dramatic. It goes up and down and up. You can walk everywhere; you don't need to use a car because you're always climbing the stairs. The Circle came out of the idea I had of downtown Zürich, which has many mixed-use shops. The buildings have flexible programs, and it is easy to change from house to hotel. My idea for The Circle was to easily create connections, much like a medieval city or an American city block. A city block should be not so big as to reduce connections between places, because those connections allow for change inside the building.

How do you approach the problem of ownership in shared space?

Yamamoto: Responsibility. This is very difficult to answer because each unit has a responsibility for their inside, but there is often no responsibility for the outside. The maintenance of the outside of the housing is a problem because people live inside their units. Sometimes there are companies that control maintenance. I was born in city housing. My mother worked in a pharmacy in front of our house, so my house was very small. There were many houses next to each other, but most of the houses were also shops like my mother's pharmacy. Most people had their own shop. Sometimes my mother and I would clean the front of the shop outside with the help of the neighboring shopkeepers. So, the benefit of maintenance of the place was evident to each person, because many people, including customers, would come to this space. The front of these houses were important spaces to everyone, because they were hybrids of public and private. This situation is very different from the single-family house whose responsibility is only the inside where it is very difficult to create the notion of responsibility. So this is often my question: how do we remake a single-family condition into a shared condition?

> You have stated that your goal is to design buildings that make people smile in a hundred years. How do you approach function in such buildings?

Yamamoto: This is related to Hannah Arendt's theories. She stated that the city should remain over the length of a human life. However, a person's life is only eighty years, or maybe hundred years, but the cityscape should last longer, because people are born in the city and die in the city. When people are born, the city should exist, and when they die, it should exist. There are many people who believe that their memory remains in the city because the city has existed for a long time. If my children know that I was born in that house, then I am a part of a memory attached with that house. That's very important for architecture. The city has a memory, many people share a memory of the city, and they know that it exists inside the city. I think it's very important that architecture and the memory should exist for a very long time. Unfortunately, in Japan it is very different. Every single-family house remains for only twenty-seven years, then it is destroyed and built again, because the developer would like to make a new house every time rather than maintain the existing house. This is the very opposite of Hannah Arendt's idea. I totally agree with her, that we should maintain the city for a long time. And that's where the idea comes from for wanting to make people smile in a hundred years.

COLLECTIVE
HERMAN HERTZBERGER

The Berlage Institute, which you helped found in 1990, has hosted some of the most relevant debates in contemporary architectural practice. Why was the Berlage Institute so successful as a platform for exchange?

Hertzberger: The Berlage Institute did not have a standard curriculum. It was a very small institution with a mission to engage the most recent developments in architecture through classes, lectures, conferences, and publications. It was very barebones, there was not really any staff. When we started it, we had some funds available, and so we asked people from all over the world to come and tell their story. But we were very selective in who we asked. There were all sorts of people we didn't want, and others we thought we should promote. This was especially important for our "students," who in fact were already professionals. We were not teaching simple, technical knowledge. It was a higher form of education, which involved listening to architects and designers with experience, both emerging and established. It was very international, and deliberately fostered a lot of debate. We had weeklong master classes where we invited architects to the Berlage Institute for a week so that the students could learn intensively from them and exhaust all their ideas.

You led a master class yourself at the Berlage Institute, "Open Structures," that explored the "adaptability, extension, and reprogramming of buildings." For what time span are your buildings intended to last?

Hertzberger: I think buildings should be more universal and not have shapes and forms based on specific programs. Most architects derive specificity from the program, which is wrong. The specificity of architecture can be derived from all sorts of different sources, but not from the program, because the program is going to change sooner or later. This is a structuralist idea. I believe we should make buildings the way we make cities, which have the quality of constant change. The city is a living organism. The buildings in the city are always changing. I have always said that S. R. Crown Hall is a very universal building. It is very good to be back here and observing all the Mies van der Rohe features, because I have always thought that Mies van der Rohe was both dull and sophisticated. A sophisticated dullness, I would say. But, when Wiel [Arets] and Vedran [Mimica] are gone and there comes a decline in the architecture school, it could also successfully be turned into anything else, including housing. A Mies van der Rohe building is so universal that it can potentially become housing, a neighborhood center, a medical center, a primary school, or a library. S. R. Crown Hall is perfectly appropriate for all those programs. It's a sort of building's building. Too many architects are suffering from the idea that they should make a building of broad gestures and dramatic effect—very wide, or narrow, or protruding—for a short-term cycle. A perfect example of universal architecture would be industrial buildings that are good for any number of other things. In fact, S. R. Crown Hall is a sort of sophisticated industrial building. There is also the famous Lingotto Factory in Torino, and more recently, the Apple Center in New York City. Big floors, big windows. These buildings are fit for everything. I'm not arguing that we make only industrial buildings, but I have been trying to figure out how you can make architecture with identity but without specificity.

Dutch Structuralism coincided closely with the Metabolists of Japan, and the two movements are often perceived as similar in their formal articulation and both remain valid today. How have you used the ideas of structuralism and metabolism in your work?

Hertzberger: Structuralism is the idea that you can build up a building from units of space that end up changing its function overall. In this sense it a very modern way of building. It creates the framework for the unexpected to happen. In Centraal Beheer [Apeldoorn, 1972] is an aggregation of space units that could be comprised of different types—sometimes a coffee corner, sometimes a restaurant, sometimes a classroom. Over time, it can be an office or a school, all the specific functions, such as bathrooms or staircases, are built in these space units. In fact, classical buildings have a similar quality of functioning in different ways. In my last book, *Architecture and Structuralism The Ordering of Space* [nai010, 2016], I compared four almost identical buildings on the Place Stanislas in Nancy, France, that all got different programmatic content. One became a hotel, one a museum, and so on. So, classicism also had this power, but we don't need to remake Doric, Ionic, or the Corinthian capitals. We must find a language that has its own identity. Mies succeeded in doing this. Mies was the first structuralist architect. He made S. R. Crown Hall black, gave it these steel profiles, and so on, and it procured a very strong identity as a result.

Your approach to structuralism has been about "finding the balance between definition and freedom." At what point does one know to stop defining space?

Hertzberger: I would say stop designing the moment that you think people can do it themselves. It's like asking a

HERMAN HERTZBERGER, CENTRAAL BEHEER
OFFICES, APELDOORN, THE NETHERLANDS, 1972.

teacher how far to go with educating. That feeds back to the Montessori value of can the pupil find this for themselves? Take the person who lives in a [860-880] Lake Shore Drive apartment, are they able to form their own apartment? And after they leave, is their apartment able to be reformed by a second, and a third person to make it their own? I would think within this situation lies the turning point.

> When you were awarded the 2012 RIBA Gold Medal, you were described as a "socially conscious person." What motivated you to become concerned with social issues as an architect?

Hertzberger: The term "social" is tricky, because it can refer to social justice causes or welfare systems. But it also means the togetherness of people, which I am much more concerned with. Most architects are frightened of people. They see people as something that destroys their work. I think that they rather enrich often rigid machinations by architects. Some of my interests in the social have come from photographers, like my friend Johan van der Keuken, who has always underlined such things. There is a photograph of a project I did, in which people have added a lot of kitsch pieces throughout the spaces. When I first saw that photograph I thought it was awful. But at a certain moment, I got the idea that it worked— the combination of kitsch with my neutral background. It was intended, as all my designs are, to be a structure that gives freedom to people to do what they want. I'm not going to try to take away that freedom and try to clear out the space when the photographer shows up. Instead, I was trying to make a framework to be infilled with whatever the individual wants to make it. However, I cannot say that this was the moment where I decided to become social.

Would you describe yourself as an architectural sociologist then, in the sense that you begin with a site and program and later go back to observe what happened to the actual building and how people use it?

Hertzberger: In a way, yes, but it comes from a strong interest in the behavior of people. You have to be interested when you see what people are doing or not doing. You have to observe, see, and make conclusions from that. So absolutely, I do think architecture should be more concerned with social science. You have to practice how to get along with everyone. The clients, the public works, and the entire bureaucracy.

Johanna Hertzberger: ...and in education, the parents and the students. It is very important to be as complete a person as possible.

You aim to bring people together so that they may focus on each other through design features in your buildings. How do you guide clients to accept these interventions?

Hertzberger: The first time I put a 5' by 5' block in the middle of a space to encourage social interaction was at the Montesorri School [in Delft]. They asked me, "Why would you do that? You can't use it as a large, open space anymore." Later, at the Apollo School, I designed a grand stair and the client said, "People will fall down them, we don't want these stairs." So, sometimes it's not easy because people don't believe in what you are proposing. I have constant discussions about safety. People want everything to be safe; you get sick of hearing about safety first. In my opinion, small children are not learning to become resilient in the face of danger because they are put in cotton wool. Everywhere, everything is safe. There are times when I am the loser and times when I am the winner. There are a lot of things that I have proposed that were not accepted by the client. The original block I mentioned still works extremely well, by the way.

> Are there any important movements that you recognize today?

Hertzberger: I have a lot of respect for the work of [Anne] Lacaton & [Jean Philippe] Vassal in France. I think they have found a direction which is very important. They have a semi-French constructivist style. They do not design all of the spatial conditions of some of their buildings, they design shells. This allows their clients to save money on the expensive final fit-outs of apartments that are likely to change, and put those savings back into the public areas of the architecture. If you look at the cost of buildings today, it breaks down to one third technical equipment, one third construction, and one third architectural infill, most of which is predetermined and there is only one or two percent that you do something with. When you turn that third for equipment into 10 percent, you have a gain of 20 percent. That's what they do. They reduce the space that requires air conditioning. Of course, during very cold winters the occupants must withdraw into the private areas that use energy. It's a very interesting idea. For instance, they have recently covered an old apartment building with a new façade. Given that the existing apartments were in very bad condition, too old, small, and leaking, it was very clever to simply extend the apartments and climate-condition them with this second skin. This sort of approach can be learned.

> You once stated that "still too many architects are trying to create beauty. I'm not against beauty, far from it. It is [just] not a goal to actively strive for." What is your goal in architecture today?

HERMAN HERTZBERGER, CENTRAAL BEHEER
OFFICES, APELDOORN, THE NETHERLANDS, 1972.
VIEW OF SPACE UNITS WITH INDIVIDUALIZED
FUNCTIONS.

Hertzberger: I think it's completely wrong to believe that the architect has to make something beautiful. I am not saying that things should not be beautiful—it could be very beautiful and at the end architecture should be beautiful, but architects should not say they want to make something beautiful. Things should be made the way they ought to be, for other reasons, by containing the basic needs of the building and be done in a beautiful way. Beauty is a result of doing things right. I think with a rational basis for the architecture, you can create the space for romantics. This whole idea that romantics are always free is untrue. When you know classical composers such as Chopin or Schumann, who make very romantic pieces, you realize that they knew exactly what they were writing and they had the techniques. They knew the rationality of the techniques. There's no sloppiness in it, their modulations and everything is mathematically correct. Flaubert, the French writer, said, "poetry is as precise as geometry." Poetics is not living in a cloud. Poetics is that you are so precise that you find the exact right word for what you have to say. Poetics is not being sloppy with words. Poetics and aesthetics are the fruits of precision, and being precise is knowing your trade and being professional.

> In 1981, at a lecture at Sci-Arc, you were quoted as saying, "I am hopeless and lost as to what architecture is today." Has your impression of architecture changed since then?

Hertzberger: I said that in 1981, but that was a long time ago. The architecture of today is not the architecture of 1981, so I don't want to use that slogan again. Although I want to ask you, why architecture? What is the sense of architecture? Does architecture contribute only to a developer's desire to maximize square-meters. That's the question we must ask ourselves. Are we making it beautiful, or more practical? What, in fact, is it that we are doing? I mean a medical doctor makes people better. He knows their sickness and gives them medicine to make them better. In what way are architects doing something that should be done? As a student of architecture, what you have to do every day is ask yourself, "What am I doing and why?"

If we look at the size of skyscrapers or new forms of urban planning, we've made technological advancements that have changed the relationship of people to space. How does your work accommodate these changes?

Hertzberger: People adapt to all sorts of situations. When you are in a skyscraper, young children have no opportunity to play in the street. But, we have no data to understand what influence that has on people. So, how can you tell me that people who are playing in the streets are different from people who are not playing in the street? I would say that I believe that it is better for your health to play in the street; you learn where the dangers are, you learn social contact with people. But I cannot prove it. I believe that the life of people, of small children, is better when they are not too high up. With the exception of the roof of the Marseille Unité [d'Habitation] by Le Corbusier, which is the most fantastic place where children can play, fight, sleep, and do everything.

Johanna Hertzberger: And not one child has ever fallen over the edge.

Hertzberger: Exactly, they have a high protective edge. The ground level also has shops and everything where people meet each other. The people know each other so well because they are in constant contact with one another. There is contact with others all over the building. It's a little bit like a market, where you have the same people coming over from the neighboring houses to shop together. These are all very important things. There is an influence, but no science to measure that influence. That should be done, but the problem is how? It becomes difficult to do as the years pass. You would have to compare between people in their youth on the fiftieth floor with children who have been playing on the street level. How can you find that out?

> A part of the new curriculum at IIT is about trying to find ways to improve the city or the metropolis...

Hertzberger: But can you do that? You can maybe trace the lines, but the city is produced by the authorities and today they don't believe the architects and the urbanists anymore. For instance, there was a time in the 1930s in The Netherlands where the authorities were listening to the urbanists. They would say, "These urbanists know how to expand the city and what to avoid doing." This time is clearly over. We must find ways to explain things to the authorities so that they believe us, and follow us with action in the ways we propose. That is the problem of today, not just the commercial clients. I think it's time to redefine what the task of an architect is or could be.

> In your career, you have simultaneously been a writer, designer, and pedagogue. Which role do you believe has had the largest impact on architecture?

Hertzberger: It's only when you are able to combine them all that you can exert the greatest force on the field. The combination of writing and practicing architecture is very important, because only then can you make us believe in what you write. Without practice, your writing can be doubted or dismissed. You may think of teaching as giving away your ideas and techniques, but it actually

AMPHITHEATRE, ARLES, FRANCE. HERTZBERGER
UTILIZES THE IDEA OF THE COLLECTIVE
CONTAINER IN HIS OWN WORK TO ARGUE FOR
AN ARCHITECTURE THAT IS ABOUT COLLECTIVE
SOCIAL SPACE AND NOT TYPE-FORM.

forces you to articulate what you are thinking. Teaching was my launch pad into writing. I would write down what I taught in school and it lead to a publication that ended up before different audiences. That's how *Lessons for Students in Architecture* [010, 1991] was born. So, it's about being able to move easily between all three roles rather than inhabiting one extremely well. The generation that I was a part of saw architecture as this way of living.

> As a leading figure in architectural education for over half a century, what are your thoughts on the changing task of formal education in the development of an architect?

Hertzberger: Education is equally consequential for both the teacher and the student. I would say that architects who are not concerned with educating the new generation are far too focused on satisfying their egos. Myself, I am a product of a Montessori education, and I've found that much of what I do in architecture involves a similar process of guided exploration. It is not something I do consciously, but I have clearly transmitted this educational attitude into my practice. The Montessori idea is to guide students in what they are already doing, rather than telling them what to do—my wife can tell you more, she was a teacher at a Montessori school. This way of teaching is not necessarily about encouraging independent decision-making, but has more to do with learning empathy. Being conscious of what others are thinking or feeling helps you explain to them what your ideas are. I want to stress that ideas are not present until they are explained, and they have to be reformulated constantly. So although formal education matters, learning happens throughout a career. Newer generations have very different views of the world. It's important to pay attention to these developments and adjust the old ways of doing things.

What mindset or attitude do you think students are most in need of adopting today?

Hertzberger: I would encourage them to rethink the mentality of needing to make very big buildings. All students want to make monuments for themselves! This idea should be removed from architectural education. The drive toward sole authorship should be erased as well. In music schools, the students are all educated to be the grand soloist that will play the violin concerto of Beethoven on every stage, even though less than one in a million will attain those positions. But budding musicians at least train to play together in an orchestra, whereas architectural education is entirely directed towards the notion of the individual genius. It is based far too much on stardom. Stars will emerge regardless. I would suggest instead that education be directed more toward the practical and historical side of architecture. Students should have an attitude towards history. How many students do you see today discussing Bernini's colonnade at St. Peters Basilica, or the Piazza dell'Anfiteatro in Lucca, and the architectural gesture of embracing people? History and the study of precedents has been completely lost in our schools. I cannot stress enough how critical these are.

Do you have any recommendations for the faculty or students at IIT to consider to enhance our discourse?

Hertzberger: Wiel is doing very well! I am inclined to say that the assignments that students are given are extremely important. Also, that the scale at which the students are designing should range from the urban design of large-scale cities to very small projects, such as designing a large staircase. Too many student curriculums focus on the design of cultural institutions—a museum, then a gallery, and then another museum again. So, I think larger design studies are good for education and discourse, because they result in more extensive analysis being conducted. Students also learn how to structure ideas in an orderly fashion. Smaller design studies, on the other hand, are important because students can get deep into the details. I was just at a meeting in the Netherlands addressing the issue that dwellings are too expensive nowadays. The whole program of housing there is completely flat, it doesn't exist anymore. With the decline in earning potential, and worries about keeping their jobs, no bank who will finance most mortgages. This is very serious. The social housing program—for which the Netherlands was famous—has also completely collapsed, because they put social housing in the hands of investors and developers. And so, an important assignment to take on for the future is to design very compact, small houses. Not 80–120 square meters, but 40–60 square meters. We will be able to find out what lifestyle is possible in such a small setting.

You are open about having a social agenda, yet you often conceal the messages in your work so that they are not immediately apparent. Why is this important to do?

Olaf: The subtexts in my work always grow very naturally. I do not start with the thought of putting secret messages into my photography. I am also not interested in being overtly political in a one-dimensional way. But, I do want people to question their initial assumptions of what the work is about as they continue to look at it, and they are slowly pulled in. The work should allow the viewer to recompose the messages, and generate new angles from which to perceive them. Photography, as a medium, is something that we have become used to. The eye so easily accepts the beautiful, the disturbing, or the journalistic. My goal is to add layers of intrigue, letting people dig deeper and ask more questions, rather than offering straightforward answers. There should be a dialogue, or a conversation. In this regard, there is no difference between my personal and commercial work, except the constraints that are unique to each assignment.

If all your work is personal, including your commercial work, how do you situate the personal in relation to the field of photography?

Olaf: I believe that whether you are an artist or architect, your work should always be personal. With seven billion people on this earth, you must stay very close to your personality and character in order to contribute anything to culture. Otherwise, your work has no use; it may as well not exist. Anyone could do it. The messages that are placed into the work should be about what moves you at that moment. This can change throughout one's life, so that in the end the artist's or photographer's body of work reads like a diary. It does not matter what it is—your aesthetics, political opinions, or youth—it should be in there.

> How do you understand the personal in terms of quality?

Olaf: There are instances when you do not understand the quality of something, or have completely different opinions about quality. That can add to our world also; as long as you recognize and have your signature. In my early work, my signature is extremely strong because I was insecure, lacked confidence, and perhaps did not understand or have full knowledge of quality. The signature must be present, but it can become a negative if expressed too strongly. In my early work, when I photographed someone in a hat, or a woman with gloves, sitting on a dustbin, I would always question myself as I was not confident in my ability.

> Can you speak a little more about the personal in your work?

Olaf: That is a very deep question; I still don't know a great deal about who I am. There was a television program in the Netherlands that asked me to do a three-hour segment. I thought three hours was a huge amount of time, and that it became incredibly personal. During the program, I almost cried and was often quite angry, yet I later found out that a reviewer thought that I was "rather shallow." This is an example that explains why, even now, when I first meet someone, or look into the mirror, I see riddles.

> Are you still searching for who you are? And if so, is it possible to find yourself in your work?

Olaf: I think everybody creates to find themselves. Except I don't want to sit around and think about it, I would rather make something while I am finding out who I am. I became internationally known in 1998 for a photograph I did for Diesel Jeans—it depicted an old lady grabbing an old man by the balls. That picture went on to win many major awards, and my career as an advertising photographer skyrocketed. There were the little things I tried to do, but these proposals were always rejected by the campaigns. For all of my projects, I have always tried to have the most multiracial and multicultural cast possible. The international advertising industry was dominated by the white race until twenty years ago which I always thought was so stupid. In the United States, or even in Asia and Africa, campaigns wanted models with blonde hair and blue eyes. I saw the change, and wanted my personal opinions to be reflected in the advertising world. So it is difficult to say if my work would suggest who I am and what I think, because those two things can be quite different sometimes.

> Your work seeks to provoke discourse through the issues you have chosen to address. How do you select the issues in relation to each project and particular moment in time?

Olaf: There are certain circumstances where you have the money and the opportunity to create a personal project. There are other moments in time where there is a need to create something personal. Most of the time it starts with a contour, one line, or one word that I picked up from watching trash television on the couch, which I find very inspirational. I meditate while people on television are fighting. Other times, such as during a delay at the airport, I try to read the subtle body languages of the waiting people around me. Waiting [2014] became a very important project, which grew from the idea that we no longer want to wait, as we are always connected. Despite the sharp rise in the population, increasingly we have less contact with each other, not more. Where twenty years ago we were waiting for the bus or an airplane, now we wait by pretending to have countless virtual friends that we connect with through the interface of a screen. While we wait, our bodies and expressions are somewhere between dead and alive. This became the starting point for the project, as it is part of our society. I have also always had a technical aspect to my research, and it is here where photography ends and film starts. An example of this would be a photo series I created, where the camera slowly pans into a restaurant in which a woman is waiting. I filmed her for three-quarters of an hour, and in that time the woman's body and facial expression collapses as she "waits" in the artificial surroundings. The conversation with the viewers, as they watch and wait to see what happens, is important for me. With film, I can decide how long it takes the viewer to understand the story. These aspects are only ever designed to help the viewer start to ask questions; I never give answers.

> Your Royal Blood [2000] series was criticized for using the language of high fashion, which was apparently insufficient to comment on the depth of the human condition. Can you comment on this?

Olaf: I think this was related to the question of technique. The Royal Blood series was accused of using the techniques of fashion photography to talk about social issues, but this was not the case; there was no social issue. The techniques that were used were chosen to comment on simply an interesting issue. I try to use the techniques that are uncommon and experimental. With this subject, I was really interested in our adoration of violence and youth. This series was about the beauty of young skin, blood, and violence. In 2000, I became increasingly interested in Photoshop so I explored that technique. I was also exploring the technique of photographing white on white at the same time. In my opinion, it was not using the technique of fashion photography. In Russia, this series was seen as my best project, yet elsewhere it was not received well. The people who connect with my work tend to be from countries with strong theatrical cultures, such as Russia, Spain, Italy, and sometimes France. I also have to hide my messages more with Anglo-Saxon cultures, as they have difficulties with sexuality and theatrics.

> Advertising's shock value, with borrowed credibility from high art, is characteristic of your work. How has the shock-factor been used in your work over the years?

Olaf: [Laughs] I am a child of 1970s Europe. Robert Mapplethorpe and Joel-Peter Witkin were the first photographers I really paid attention to. My shock value is nothing; in comparison to them, I am just a soft ball of cotton. My early work wasn't made for the world, it was made for myself and my group of friends. Coming from a little town, Utrecht, I was very surprised that my first friends at art school were already posing nude. I started out as a journalistic photographer, but realized that I preferred connecting with people in the Amsterdam nightlife. Then I withdrew from active participation in the nightlife and started photographing characters from the nightlife in my studio; these were often staged scenes of my fantasy. There was a door lady I had heard about who had beaten up five boys. I thought if she could do that, she could also lift a boy over her head. I approached her with this idea, but she agreed on the condition that she would be nude. So the nudity actually came from her. I was following the mentality of my peers. When my photos went public, many international audiences said that it was shock pho-

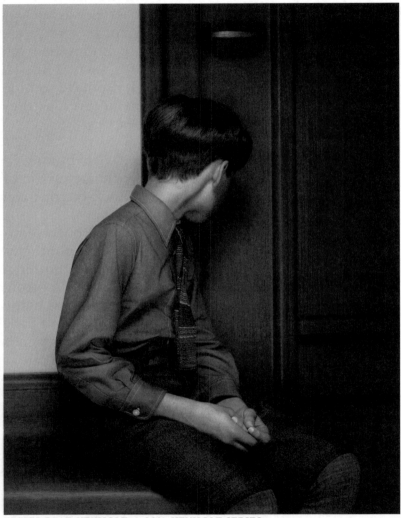

ERWIN OLAF, KEYHOLE#1, 2011. KEYHOLE SERIES.
CHROMOGENIC PRINT.

tography. The photograph of a fake Princess Diana from the Royal Blood series was also extensively commented on in the English and Australian newspapers. People called me an asshole, but for me it was only a coincidence and a joke. You can never forecast what will happen to a project. As soon as you plan to make a shock photo, you make it shit or kitsch. I have always made pictures based on who I am, and at that moment in time I was angry and partly naïve. A lot of people tend to get hung up on the body, skin, and sex, but it is just who we are.

> While you may not have done it purposely, can this technique be seen as a critique of today's image-based culture and culture of consumption?

Olaf: A big change has come about with the digital age. Many people now use shock value to get attention. Those pictures were made in my youth when I was still quite naïve. I am still very influenced by my youth. My mentality towards the body and sex comes from my upbringing in the 1970s, not from a desire for shock value. I would not use the same approach that I used in the 1980s as I have lost my naiveté. I now know better than to simply shock, as that makes it empty and kitsch. I execute my ideas in my mind, and if it turns out to be shocking to someone, it is a pity. I never want to shock people. In Skin Deep [2015], I came back to the subject of skin and the body after twenty-five years, because it was always so misunderstood. I wanted to make something that showed my love for the human form and movement. I see no need to hide the genitals of the model if the composition of the photo is good.

> Is the inclusion of other mediums in your work complementary to photography, or an answer to its limitations?

Olaf: It is just my research process. I have made sculptures with a 3D camera and then sent them off to be made physically to scale by the Carrara industries. That is a kind of photography to me as well. The other thing to ask is, how do we display our work? Is it to build an architecture, or a triangular projection? Or is it to make a montage, and experience of viewing the work? It gets boring for me nowadays to just make photographs. So in the upcoming Hotel de Ville project, I am morphing sets of photo projections, along with ultra-slow motion films. I am doing this to keep myself interested in the field of photography. It is also something different from making beautiful pictures without meaning.

> This is a good moment to talk about framing a photograph. There are size constraints with older technology, and nowadays, people want their images to be bigger. How much does size matter?

Olaf: I have just rebuilt my darkroom to go back to printing in black and white. I love the combination of old and new techniques. Two years ago, I made portraits of the Jewish communities in Amsterdam. I had taken the photos digitally, but I printed them using carbon printing, which is one of the oldest techniques. Before I began this project I had seen carbon prints in the drawers of the Getty Museum. They were so beautiful; it was as if they were printed yesterday. In Amsterdam, about nine-tenths of the Jewish population were taken away in the Second World War, so I wanted a way for these photos to last forever, which turned out to be carbon printing. One type of carbon print was limited in size and took one or two days to make, as it was so delicate. I tried it out, but I didn't want to do that for the rest of my life. Then I thought of the silver-bromide printing that I had done for many years, until the 1990s. So I reintroduced silver-bromide back into my studio. It is very meditative, and far more tactile and emotional to look at. I have just obtained a digital enlarger that enables me to print silver-bromide with digital photos, combining new and old; although you are still limited in size, so I suppose sizes do matter.

> Your work has navigated both high art and low art. Which best captures your audience?

Olaf: I never know my audience. Do architects know their audience? This afternoon, I was in Chicago's Museum of Contemporary Art (MCA) when a student recognized me. I was surprised as I thought he was too young to know my work. At an opening of an exhibition in Italy once, several older ladies were in attendance because I had made a series with mature ladies as pin-up models. In Italy, they have an appreciation for the older women as sex symbols. As an artist, all my work must be produced in absolute freedom. This is the reason I work in advertising; I save my money from my assignments and every one and a half years I make my own project. With absolute freedom, you can have your own signature and that in turn will foster a market. It has worked for me until now.

> Your highly stylized photography focuses on the general notion of "beauty" in order to draw in the viewer. How can beauty be made so objective?

Olaf: Beauty is incredibly subjective! In my opinion, there is a general, median opinion of what beauty is that I often subscribe to for my series. Grief was a series that uses beauty to bring people into my world. It is about a life's first tear. I wanted to tell a fairytale about sorrow. The work relies heavily on beautiful architecture and beautiful women, who are reacting to terrible news. The series drags you into my world in this beautiful setting, which then shatters as I slap you across the face with tragedy. I wanted to add something different to the photographic discourse, as there is already so much sorrow in this world. That series made me realize that I have matured, and I do not need to rely on so many arguments to make a beautiful photograph.

> It is clear that your work is about how you orchestrate these fantasy worlds. Which films or film directors have had the greatest influence on you?

Olaf: I am very influenced by Italian movies from the 1970s. [Lucino] Visconti and [Pier Paolo] Pasolini were both very strong figures. Also, Jacques Tati's *Playtime*, with its play on aesthetics, and Douglas Sirk's tearjerkers, with their beautiful compositions. I have lost track of the directors nowadays, so I prefer to search a little bit further away from home. I have also tried to stay away from other photographers in order to maintain my originality. Without that, I would think that everything has already been done. I have always adored Visconti's precision, although the aesthetics in the older films were sometimes so overwhelming that sometimes the acting suffered. Nowadays, I tell myself to go deeper into the acting and less into the aesthetics.

> Many photographers try to be pure in their use of the medium. Your photos are all manipulated, much like the manufactured world of film. Would you agree?

Olaf: Yes, it is true that film is one of my largest sources, but I am also interested in theater. Nowadays, my work is about what adds to the stories of our lives. How do the details, such as the distance between the phone and the furniture, or whether the model is cross legged or not, enhance the story-telling? For example, in the Rain [2004] and Hope [2005] series, which were based on the aesthetics of the 1950s in America, there are details in each set that add up to a narrative. The action-reaction moments after the Western world was paralyzed by the news of 9/11, for instance. My aim was to create something very positive, similar to a Norman Rockwell landscape, in order to celebrate the good times of American freedom. The set was organized around teenagers in a dance hall, but it was so terribly kitsch. At a certain point I told them to stop dancing so that I could take my shot. It was the moment between action and reaction. I disagree that I am only interested in beauty, I think that everybody is beautiful. Many times in documentary photography, human forms that have been distorted such as obese bodies are studied and thus humiliated. But I am not interested in that, I think there is beauty in everybody.

> How does detaching your audience from current times, with references to the past, allow you to better discuss contemporary issues?

Olaf: I am now slowly finding my interests in our present time. In Keyhole [2011–13], whose images could be from the 1920s, or similarly timeless settings, my starting point was the idea of our disconnection from one another. We are here at this moment listening to me speak, but elsewhere there are people making love, having a fight, or perhaps stabbing each other. However, we neither know nor care who they are. I wanted to discuss that phenomenon, yet when it is set in the present time, it gets too personal. I built this elaborate set of rooms next to each other using the beautiful aesthetics of the 1920s. While on set shooting, I saw a little boy who was so bored from waiting that he would look through the keyholes into the other sets to amuse himself. I thought, this was it! The keyhole allowed the boy to look into another world from his own point-of-view. So the final installation forces the

ERWIN OLAF, SQUARES, POWERLIFTING, 1985.

audience to peek through two keyholes, and see a man or a woman holding a young boy on his or her lap. The question being, what happens in our minds when we see the two figures doing exactly the same thing, from the keyhole perspective of an unwanted onlooker? The scene extends deeper when the aesthetics are detached from our time. The aesthetics also provide more layers to the piece, and translate the subject into something far more intriguing and poetic. The more layers a piece of art has, the longer people will be intrigued by it.

> There seems to be a certain logic behind the naming of your pieces: Keyhole, Rain, Hope, and Waiting.

Olaf: It is very much like writing the first sentence of a story. I try to provoke the audience to start thinking about waiting. My earlier work had messages, but now I want to have dialogues. The title is the first entrance into the work. Making them short makes them more open, which I like.

> Waiting is interesting, as it is double entendre. It is also about the viewers waiting for the film to end?

Olaf: Yes. Nowadays I want to tease, not to shock, so that the audience starts to think. A photo editor once said to me that a beautiful picture is totally unimportant, explaining that thousands of pictures are produced each day with beautiful landscapes and people. However, such photos are incredibly shallow. I was just at Anish Kapoor's Cloud Gate sculpture. It is beautiful at first sight, but I was more intrigued by the city as it was reflected in its form. Beauty by itself is such a boring subject; it should be used to start a much deeper discussion. I don't believe that reality must be attached with ugliness, the point is to study and do more research. I think that I am at the end of a cycle, and maybe the next stage of my career will be uglier and more in the here and now.

> Can you talk a little bit more about how shooting, almost exclusively, in constructed sets helps your agenda beyond the issue of control?

Olaf: It gives me the ability to tell the story more precisely. The inside of any character that you see is built up from the outside. I completely control the surroundings to add to the person, or an action the audience is viewing. I can move walls, and furniture, to control the atmosphere surrounding the lives of those characters. There is a quality of silence in the sets that cannot be found in reality, which allows me to speak. There is also no time constraint in controlled environments. In real locations, you have to be very convinced about what you are doing prior to entering the location, but I often need more time, because I sometimes don't know what I want out of the project. Although, having just worked on location in Berlin, I might be at the end of this cycle. The high ceilings and decorative details in the buildings of Berlin allowed me to easily create the lighting I had in my mind.

> Perhaps you can talk about the use of a fantasized reality? How does that help with the message?

Olaf: Nobody is in my way, I look at a blank sheet of paper and imagine the whole image. The space, the objects, and the light. I can change the curtains, I can think about the kinds of flowers, and I can think about how the direction and intensity of light adds to the emotion. Even the conflicts between the carpet and wallpaper can be used to tell the story of a lady "waiting." I can imagine the context outside of the scene that adds to a story of loneliness. Even the sounds of the film and the materials in the surroundings help the viewer to locate a person, as well as the whole atmosphere and mood of the story. Having to search for a place that has all the elements precisely as I have them in my mind is far too difficult. It is just far easier for me to construct these sets. However, I do get my ideas from real places, such as the Hilton Hotel I am at today. I studied the room, the people, the breakfast, and the new broom the housecleaner had. A broom should never be new!

> In the Berlin [2012] series, did you realize anything profound during the experience of shooting on site?

Olaf: Yes, I think the setting added a new depth that I have not found in my studio for twenty years. It made the photography much richer. The story was changing as we shot on location; it became much darker. Berlin is about the interbellum years in Europe, between the First and Second World Wars. I wanted to explore the time in Europe where a dark thunder cloud was coming towards it; perhaps we are now in a kind of interbellum also. I only wanted to work in buildings that existed during the interwar years. The atmosphere in the buildings really absorbed the crew. The lighting was much darker than when I sketched it out in my mind; the wooden panels and concrete also made it moodier. The stairs in the indoor swimming pool had so many angles to choose from, making it so much richer than working in the studio. Berlin was the most expensive project I have ever made; I could only afford it because I won the Netherlands state prize for the arts [Johannes Vermeer Award, 2011]. I would like to do more poetic projects about cities in transition, perhaps in Detroit or Shanghai.

> Can you talk more about the Hotel de Ville [L'Éveil, 2016] project you did for Nuit Blanche

in Paris? Can an intervention in a very large hotel be considered an intervention at the urban scale?

Olaf: I think so. The project I did for Nuit Blanche is now on tour in Paris, along with many other artists, like Anish Kapoor and Matthew Barney. To me, Paris is a beaten city. You feel it in the mentality. My feeling is that the artists and audience that will visit Paris will still expect something similar to the recent tragedies to occur. My message is to simply say, well, we are still gathered here. I am projecting fifteen bodies of different size and color. Who'd have thought, I started out with nudity and here I am again with lots of nudity. My aim is to have my projection wake up the festival. It is a three-minute loop of church bells ringing, after which the building comes alive with the projected bodies unfolding, until finally they rest in the political position of extending their arm upwards. For me it is a new step, as now all art appears to be shifting, and influencing each other; architecture and photography especially, due to the fact that buildings often survive through photographs. How important is photography in architecture?

Very. It is also about who is photographing your work. When you talk about an architect, you always think about their photographer as well, as they are so strongly connected to the work. Iwan Baan photographs everything, but he is now the biggest name in architectural photography.

Olaf: It's also difficult, because nobody knows about your beautiful buildings if there are no photos from a certain angle. There are ugly and good angles in architecture, or can you also have a building that is good from every angle? Everything has a beautiful angle in my opinion.

The question is who the photographer is.
Some buildings are known because a good
photo was taken of it. Sometimes you only
need one picture, so that when you think of a
building you only think of that iconic picture.
Olaf: Yes. Imagine if the photographer did not take that
photo, then the building would not exist in that way. I
designed a new Euro coin because we had a new king.
The material and stamping was very new and unfamiliar
to me, and at a certain point, because of time constraints,
I had to stop designing and the coin was produced as it
was. I never saw the real thing before the production,
and there was only one chance for me to iterate the design, which was stupid. But the most important thing
was the successful reception of the 3D rendering from
the Dutch public. It was this image that was imprinted
into the public's minds. I had a sentence for the concept
describing how the design came from the diamond cuts,
and also the Dutch landscape, which was printed in every newspaper along with the 3D rendering, and people
really liked it. Yet when the coin was in everyone's hand,
you realize, "Oh, is this all?"

DAVID ADJAYE

> You approach architecture as a multiplicity of ideas, from place-making to the role of light and sun, it being an object as well as a social act, responding to local culture, climate, and geography while being part of a global community. You seem not to have a single, unified position.

Adjaye: I take these positions because the conditions of the city and the societies we live in demand such a response. There are fundamentals that are always at work, but these fundamentals are not concrete for me. They are instead ideological, and positioned in such a way that one is able to test them against different conditions. That might be the time that we are in, but I find that testing process very stimulating, as well as the results that it produces.

> Architecture is typically conceived as a slow-moving practice, tasked with providing shelter, stability, and security. Yet, you see it as fluid and able to deal with a multiplicity of design approaches, of plurality of cultures, and of the rupturing into multiple spectrums.

Adjaye: This complexity is the rich soup that an architect like myself very much enjoys. The twentieth century created a rupture in the singular narrative of the modern, and unraveled the multiplicity of moderns that were happening all over the world. Architecture has been late to that discussion. Contemporary art, as being the first to understand and to pursue that rupturing, has had many successes in being relevant and responsive in the world. Architecture is finally starting to crack and explore this, which creates a very rich potentiality spectrum for the twenty-first century.

> Adolf Loos said that, "art does not belong in architecture," which has been the general consensus in the past decades, yet you talk about architectural practice as part of, or even following art practices.

Adjaye: There's been an end to big grand statements and so I don't find that statement too relevant. There's an exploration that's happening across all platforms and a freedom from feeling that any dogma has any kind of specific power. I think that this sense of freedom to explore in this time creates strange monsters and very interesting projects. From it, synthesis happens and direction always finds a way out.

The idea of the practice as a philosophical and intellectual inquiry is fascinating. What artists have been able to do is achieve a certain freedom, which architects continually lose. We tend to write it out of our own scripts because we don't quite have a way of making it a language the way artists do. There's a precise power that artists have about the relevance of what they do. We can articulate it, but very few can stand being it, so it became very interesting for me to just collaborate with artists to further explore this notion.

At the beginning, it had to do with the school I went to, the Royal College of Art: discussing ideas and hearing their position, seeing the uncompromising nature in which they were able to behave, that architects could not; it brought about this fascination with the field. I wanted to understand the basis of their particular convictions. It started off as dialogues in bars, and eventually became collaborations around the potential they could unleash on architecture. It's become very fluid now; I don't insist on collaborating with artists, but when I do I'm happy to be working with individuals that don't have preconceived ideas about what they think art/architecture is. Because it's not just about art or architectural practice, but about being able to explore, right now, and not have any boundaries.

> What are the characteristics of architecture that lend themselves to this boundary-free world?

Adjaye: The wonderful thing about architecture is that it's always been an exchange mechanism, since its beginning. It's one of the most fluid knowledge systems. I think when lessons are learned, they quickly move to different places, and when techniques or forms are perfected, they quickly migrate because they're successful. In our time, there's the obvious of how technology migrates, but also how we migrate. The speed at which people migrate moves the knowledge of architecture. Also, it challenges the nature of architecture, the speed at which it can respond.

> You speak of migration of people, and as it applies to your situation, having lived in many different countries, you say it has helped you to not take any location as being the norm. What are these norms?

Adjaye: There are habits that come from having a singular sense of the importance of place. That is romantic. It also just has to do with time; there's a durational relationship that creates habits and patterns, which are the norms that I'm talking about. Most people have them.

> How then do you see the making of a place in relation to time and duration?

DAVID ADJAYE, SMITHSONIAN NATIONAL
MUSEUM OF AFRICAN HISTORY AND CULTURE,
WASHINGTON, DC, 2016. WORM'S EYE PERSPEC-
TIVE OF THREE-TIERED FORM, INSPIRED BY THE
YORUBAN CARYATID.

Adjaye: Place-making is the essential thing that we do and that I'm interested in. I would almost say that place-making is more important to me than buildings. It's about being able to concretize the information that creates a certain citizenry in a society or in a city. It's also an attempt to make sense of how architecture can speak to a message about a certain time. The specificity of a time, frozen in the architecture, is something I enjoy. It's not something that I find problematic. I don't find it necessary to find timelessness. In fact, I find timelessness too abstract for my brain to even comprehend. People use that word so easily, so casually, and I don't even know what it means. I'm more interested in trying to find a resolution, which captures the place in its time.

> In your work, do you design for specific norms as related to place and time, or does your position as a nomad having no ingrained norms, tend to make you reject the typical expectations?

Adjaye: It's interesting, because I never really enjoy architecture that attempts to completely script the way in which life happens. I like architecture that frames and surprises. I'm speaking specifically about public life, because that's the loosest form. The private home can be highly scripted because it's a really powerful set of profiles: sleeping, sitting, eating, cooking, bathing. Public life becomes richer when architecture creates frames rather than when it orchestrates a narrative.

> What has the role of your research on Africa played in your understanding of architecture?

Adjaye: When I was doing my research into Africa, it was an attempt to fundamentally understand the nature of nation-making and the emergence of the moderns. In particular, to understand the stories.

Rem Koolhaas's project with Lagos was interested in the mutations of a city, and the particularity of those mutations. That was a project he'd been doing for a very long time in different places and Lagos was one iteration. Iwan Baan and Manuel Herz's recent project is a very interesting one, tracking European modernism, its infiltration into Africa, and the mutation that happens when it hits Africa.

My research was about simply not forgetting that there's this incredible continental plate, which birthed fifty-three ideas of the modern. Whether failing or not, there is an attempt to create these fifty-three modern states, ideas and identities.

Ultimately, my analysis after twelve years of being with this information, was profound to me, but also reinforced an age-old thinking about architecture. That, in the end, even with a very strong political or ideological idea, architecture must create a narrative in which the work reacts to the ground, and to the patterns. It seems crazy to take twelve years to know something that you already know, but in a way, it took that closer look to understand it in a way that was very substantive and immovable for me. This concept was no longer ideological; it was very much a printed fact in my mind.

The narrative of how I worked was always imbued with this idea, this sensibility. Subconsciously, I was always searching for it. In my early London work I was trying to find a "London-ness", or a particular east-end quality. But, I realized that what I was actually looking for was a particular island architecture, more than a "London-ness." It's a dreamer architecture scenario. The more I tried to look for "London" architecture, the more it didn't work for me anymore. Now, somebody could read it differently and say, "No, this is very particularly London," but I'm skeptical if that information is actually useful as a way of understanding how to make architecture.

What I'm interested in very much now, which Africa taught me, is how a return to the fundamentals offers a lens to see hybridity and mutations as particularities within the context of a bigger diagram rather than as just for their own sake. It returns us to a planetary discourse, rather than a global discourse. Rather than an ideological orientation, it is a physical one. It is extremely physical, about forces and resistance, which I found very powerful.

> You were born to Ghanaian parents, and you now have your office in Accra. Why did you set up the office there, and what do you believe you could do for Africa?

Adjaye: Accra is very much an ideological setup. Traveling around the continent, it became clear to me that, 90 percent of the time, the way the built environment is being made omits the art of architecture. "Aid architecture" and the kind of "you should be grateful" thinking from the 1980s to now has created a warped, distorted, mutated sense of what modern can be on the continent. Young African kids tear it apart and mutate it into other things; they don't have the ability to absorb it, because they feel it's fake. There's implicitly a feeling that it's not theirs, but they don't have any other alternative. By looking at the imagery, and comics coming from these incredibly diverse and smart kids, it's clear that the tearing apart and destroying is because of that absence. What I'm very keen to see, and what I'm starting to postulate examples of, is architecture that has a luxury and a precision, an enjoyment of place, which has been lacking for a long time in these amazing geographies. There's a kind of foundational sense to this project, because the modernization of Africa starts with a repositioning of modern

DAVID ADJAYE, FRANCIS A. GREGORY NEIGHBOR-
HOOD LIBRARY, WASHINGTON, DC, 2012.
REFLECTIVE, DIAMOND-GRIDDED FACADE THAT
DISAPPEARS INTO THE SURROUNDING PARK.

technology to the continent and a slight adjustment related to the fundamental problem of climate and cultural
tropes. There's a defamation of modernity, but there isn't
a moment of using technology and enjoying the luxury of
the place. There are very few examples that I know of, but
when they do appear, they're very powerful. In this way, I
think the continent can make very powerful architecture,
and I'm very interested in and excited about that.

> You reference a lot of African artifacts when
> talking about your projects, while also want-
> ing your architecture to go beyond the idea of
> the object. Do these artifacts serve as physical
> or mental starting points for your work?

Adjaye: I specifically reference a lot of artifacts, but not
to make simulacrums or to find fundamental reductions.
I think that there's something about the period of time
coming out of the medieval, or even predating that—Nok
architecture goes back 3,000 years, for example—in which
the civilizations on the continent used abstraction as a very
powerful coding device. They were representing notions of
society, enclosure, and adornment.

There was also a separation from nature;
even though there was a simulating and playing with
nature, I consistently found an abstraction that really
spoke about man's articulation of his environment—
right through to the most mundane objects. This is
pre-technology, pre-industrialized technology even,
and there's this human element in trying to create ab-
stractions which speak to something more. I've been
fascinated with looking back at these objects, almost
like pieces of technology. For me, they're not romantic, at all; they're real. They present systems: sometimes
they are literal systems, like an approach to dealing
with a mundane condition of industrialization, which
I find problematic. Sometimes they are messages about

understanding how to deal with environmental strategy. They're very powerful for me.

Also, they decouple me from known knowledge, from my literature. I have a fantastic library of books, and I know them all, and I know all the references in them, but I want the work to go beyond this. When I know the reference very literally, I'm very worried with my work—I don't like it. I try to go past the references that I know, usually by entering a different realm that allows me to shake my own comfort zone, and it becomes about continually using objects, or textiles, or pieces to question what I know and myself. It's a strange thing—not about literacy, but inspiration too.

> You see the practice as a platform for inquiry. So, do you follow the general architectural discourse or do you try to push it past its own preconceived notions of what it is?

Adjaye: It's a bit of both. I do pay attention because I'm aware of what's going on. But, I am very turned off by dogma or by patterns. It's intrinsically my tendency to be deeply suspicious of ingrained patterns because I think that they stop critical thinking. I've not had the opportunity to make lots of general buildings, so, I don't find myself needing established patterns as a way of working. I find myself looking for directions that may open up new possible patterns. In my work, I'm getting clients who want me to explore what their program might be as a built form, but also what that might mean as a strategy of how to make and how to position things.

Sustainability is an example. Sometimes we're within the canon, but a lot of the times we're trying to push it. But, when I'm trying to push it, I'm not really interested in the idea of sustainability as a series of mechanisms that come in, but to implicitly uncover what architectural strategies offer as sustainability. I deeply trust the instinct of the architect to produce sustainable rationale, even at its thinnest or thickest. The question is uncovering the narrative and the technologies and the strategy to make full sense of that.

> How does your practice operate to encourage questioning and exploring?

Adjaye: It's a studio. There is something beautiful about being in a studio, where the purpose is to create an environment for and an evolution of inquiry. In the studio, everyone is welcome to be part of it, in an intimate way. When I saw that model, I became completely enchanted by it: it became the model of the practice I wanted. It's the model of the practice I have.

> In 2008, during the economic downturn, you said that you had to "go big or go home." And that you went big. How has that impacted your practice?

Adjaye: By that I meant I faced a scenario where I could've just contracted and returned to a more traditional, what I call accountant or banker strategy, where we just strip everything down to the bare minimum and see if we can survive. I chose to, instead, expand my practice. It was a propulsion to go beyond and learn. I lived in a globalized condition, not a localized one, and even though there was a certain local condition in London, there were other opportunities elsewhere. It forced me to become much more nomadic in my practice, a quality that has become something I now absolutely treasure. Even through it's destabilizing in terms of my life, it's incredibly nourishing in terms of my intellectual inquiry and my ability to create and move about the world.

> Africa, Europe, and America is certainly a very interesting setup. There are not a lot of archi-

DAVID ADJAYE, SUGAR HILL HOUSING, HARLEM,
NEW YORK, 2015. VIEW OF FENESTRATION DETAIL
AND EMBOSSED "ROSE" GRAPHIC ON THE
FACADE THAT ARE DESIGNED TO BE RESPONSIVE
TO CONTEXT.

tects who have had the luxury of living in one of the most promising continents, Africa, who also live in America and in Europe. What do you see in this triangular relationship?

Adjaye: Fundamentally, I wanted to set up offices in this triad. There's a kind of triptych between that continent, America, and Europe. In Africa there is a history, a lived way, in which the life has a certain precision to do with a very intense and uncomplicated geography in its various regions. That is very difficult for other continents to understand. That kind of primary geography doesn't exist in such a fundamental way on other continental plates. During my research, I suddenly realized, it's the only continent with these strips of pure geography, which have created a very particular pattern in life. This pattern has to be experienced—it cannot be understood remotely because it doesn't have a relational code with other continents. Because I experienced that as a child, it's deeply steeped in. But then to have had a European, and later an American, education, enables me to focus on two, probably three bottles. Working in these different contexts allows me not to see any contradictions or trauma. I don't have any trauma with this triple vision.

I'm very much interested in this triangle, and you've put it in a very logical set up. You mentioned that you are living in a nomadic condition. What is home, then? Accra? Or is it London? Is it New York City?

Adjaye: This nomadic condition is one that I've settled into because I have emotional connections to the places we have discussed: Accra, London, and even New York City, now. I've been here for a decade now, but at the same time I don't really have any attachments in the roots sense.

Are you saying you have no attachments to the places you've lived in? Or worked in?

Adjaye: What I mean is that I don't fundamentally understand my identity through the place. I understand my time through the place. Like the time I spent is definitely through the lens of London, or through the lens of Accra. But I don't see it as the force that actually identifies me. I don't feel a sense of a return to it as a nourishing source pool, just nostalgia. I've had to find nourishment from a different position, one that is very nomadic. My wife, and now my son, we talk about being able to move to a different places all the time. And it's something that we now have fully embraced. It may be destabilizing for families, but it's very exciting too.

So then, can you tell us where you're from? Where is your home?

Adjaye: I can never answer that question, honestly. I always start with a narrative. I studied in London but I live now a lot in New York City, but I have a home in London, and my parents are from Ghana. I lived in Ghana, but I also lived in the Middle East, and for a very long time, in East Africa, which is where I was born. Family is probably the core. If there's a stable element, that's it. With all of its complexity. That's basically home.

What you said about these three conditions, this nomadic home, this triangle of operation; it's an ideological setup?

Adjaye: Yeah, it is an ideological setup. It's kind of also a reality! It's not trying to be a fiction. It's real.

Of course it's very real. Many of us are like you. Originally from somewhere, then working somewhere else, only to move to another place, yet somehow, always coming back to our origins. It leaves us wondering about our origins and the kind of knowledge they make relevant. To what extent can we, with an international or global knowledge, deal with the local situation? It's an interesting position; very tense as well. Do we belong there? Are we preaching? Or understanding? Or not understanding, but simply modernizing? Ultimately, it is about how this ideological setup affects us, fundamentally challenging our understanding and our operation as architects, as thinkers, even as humans.

ARMAND MEVIS

How do you position yourself in the field of graphic design?

Mevis: I have a troubled relationship with my own discipline. What I value is the purity of an idea, for instance, ideas in conceptual art. It's difficult to look at your own work and know that there are ideas in it that are meaningful to you, but are not intended for an audience. So sometimes you start to think about your work quite negatively, because you miss the possibility in this discipline to be pure and clear.

When we compare your work to conceptual art, where the idea overcomes effect, you seem to take the opposite approach, where effect is the main intention.

Mevis: We always start with an idea, meaning we try to understand the situation first, and the context. It is through this analysis of a field that we try to understand what we're actually dealing with. Then we distill an aspect that we think is interesting, or something that should be highlighted, which leads to a starting point. The activity is then focused on how to make your idea work—to transform and formalize it such that people understand what you are trying to say. That's where form becomes important as a tool to trigger your audience.

What ideology or set of principles do you make use of in order to translate the content into a graphical language?

Mevis: First of all, it would be good to understand the

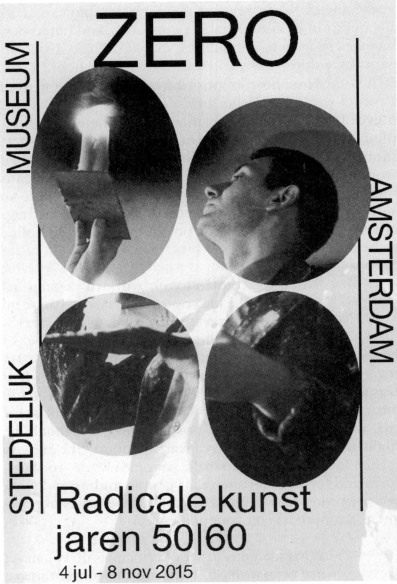

MEVIS & VAN DEURSEN, "ZERO" EXHIBITION
POSTER, STEDELIJK MUSEUM, AMSTERDAM, 2015.

term "ideology": what it could mean or what it means to everyone. The work is driven by things, by ideas, and also by ideologies. What we try to do in our discipline, is actually question its conventions, boundaries, and outcomes. Can we cross these boundaries, can we actually come up with new solutions? In other words, what is a book? What is the function of the spine of a book's cover? How does a poster work? Can a poster do the work of a book? All those kinds of questions come to mind. By questioning these things, you try to reshape the work you do, and that as an ideology can drive the work.

What kind of art inspires you?
Mevis: I like work that makes you think about something in a new way. I have problems with work that is too well made and aesthetically beautiful, because I consider that to be something than can be learned by everyone. I prefer work that makes me think. That's why I feel connected to work by artists like Ed Ruscha. For example, in the Royal Road Test [1967] with Jason Williams and Patrick Blackwell, they traveled by road to the desert with a Royal typewriter machine, which they threw out of the car, and then very seriously investigated what happened to the typewriter when it was thrown out of the car. How many meters? Did it roll? They made pictures as if they were police investigators. It was absurdness staged in a very serious manner.

Some of your work appears to be extremely straightforward, so as to be almost not designed, for example, *Wiel Arets—Bas Princen*, published by Hatje Cantz [2015]. Would you agree?
Mevis: You can choose to act in different ways, and engage yourself in different ways with a project. You understand what some projects need, for whom it is meant, and what

your role can be in that process. I have practiced for thirty years, but at the very beginning of my practice, I considered each project as an opportunity to manifest a lot of ideas, which meant many of these projects suffered from too many ideas and too much ambition. Now, I'm much more aware of that and more capable of understanding what should be done, but also what should not be done. For a book like *Wiel Arets—Bas Princen*, it was very clear what needed to happen and what my role was. The book would not work if the graphic design manifested itself too much. It would have killed the book; there are other projects where I knew that a strong, formal gesture, a very expressive gesture, was needed. I'm capable of seeing and using the opportunity to best complement the content.

In cases where it's very simple, do you see that as a commentary on contemporary culture?

Mevis: Some projects hit on things that discuss something, so you use them as examples to clarify your approach to your work. It's not that there is just one way, you can operate in different ways. You have a voice that can have different ranges and tones, and you can use them in a different manner each time to articulate something different. It's not a commentary on contemporary culture, but the exercising of a well-trained blade, exerting just the right amount of pressure or control.

Can you talk about how you exercise control through the tools you use?

Mevis: We use a limited amount of typefaces and a small set of tools, and work within a number of restrictions. It's like setting the rules of a game you want to play—you can also start to respect or disrespect those rules. But you need to have some kind of clarity, and that's why I always like to set up a situation in which the possibilities of what you can do are limited.

The means by which people receive and digest information continually changes throughout time. How does this impact your work?

Mevis: I suffer from the same barrage of information coming at me that everyone does. Because everything is information, sometimes you try to avoid it because when it's all coming at you—on the street, at an airport, ads, signage, everywhere, all the time—you get overwhelmed. Everything tries to attract your attention. For example, when you open a magazine, there are so many things all happening at the same time. It's very confusing. I try not to see it, but I don't know if that's a good way of dealing with it. There's also a lot of information that doesn't even go through the hands of designers. All the information is processed by people, but not always with the intention to solve the problem, or make things better for you. I never feel the urge to take a responsibility to improve what's out there in the environment, where good design could have a meaningful impact. It's very hard to enter this world, where things become very commercial.

What do you think of the shock factor, where it seems that only the loudest and most extreme voice will be heard?

Mevis: This is also a problem for architects. If you just walk through a city, maybe 99 percent of the buildings you don't even want to see, since they're not interesting, and even ugly. You always look for exceptions, the things that stand out. In graphic design, it's the same. There is too much information to even start thinking about wanting to change it.

In your own monograph, *Mevis & Van Deursen: Recollected Work* [Artimo, 2005] by Paul Elliman, you use images as content more so than

MEVIS & VAN DEURSEN, "POP ART" BILLBOARD
AND ENTRANCE TO THE EXHIBITION, MUSEUM
OF CONTEMPORARY ART CHICAGO, CHICAGO,
ILLINOIS, 2015.

text. How did you mediate between graphic design and content in this instance?

Mevis: When we made that book, a lot of people were disappointed, or maybe annoyed. For a book made up of images, the images were not accessible and didn't lead you to the original project, which was of course intentional. When we work with the material of others, whether an artist, a photographer, or an architect, we try to do something very specific for that person. So for our own book we also had to come up with something specific that would relate to our work. Our work can also be seen as raw material that, once printed, is reduced to colors and forms. We wanted to see if we could make new work with old work, by making new collages. All these fragments are like the leaves of a tree, and you can make compositions with them. There is a counterpart to the collages, where we talk about our relationship with clients. These accounts are very honest and very direct, and sometimes for the people whom we talk about, not very friendly. There are two things happening in the book at the same time.

The complexity of this book seems to reflect the plurality of our postmodern condition. Was capturing that part of the design intent?

Mevis: It was good for a specific purpose, so this book becomes a work in itself and not a representation of something else. The book is a one-on-one experience that happens at the moment that you actually open it. It's more like an artist's book, where it doesn't refer to anything else other than itself.

How has the role of the graphic designer changed since you first entered the discipline?

Mevis: It is becoming more interesting today, because designers have the ability to operate in more fields and areas of practice, including publishing, curating, editing, writing, image making, typesetting. In the past, when I was a student and starting out, the disciplines were more segregated. A designer would never have been able to publish, because the costs for these activities were so high. Today, my students can publish and print books because a lot of facilities are much more accessible. Books, printed in full color, offset, with fantastic paper and perfect binding, and a print run of only a hundred, making it not less important, but allowing them to operate in different fields of interest. I think that makes the profession richer. Perhaps it also marginalizes the discipline of graphic design a little, because a lot of these projects happen in a very small niche, where only those who know about that scene also know about the work that is being done, whereas it's completely invisible to the rest of the world.

Will technology further reshape the discipline? Mevis: There's an opportunity for a new generation of designers to be in greater control of new media, as well as the moving image, which can expand the discipline. The internet is no longer static, it becomes more time-based, and movie-making becomes a greater part of the practice. There are many ways to tell stories, not just in the form of a book. Today, it's often still a book, plus a version on another device, such as the iPhone or iPad. The printed version and a digital version co-exist. Those who invest in these potentials, by learning how to program and be more in control, have the best chance to thrive in the future. I come from the world of printmaking, and I am intrigued by the potential of all these new forms of media.

Different platforms require different forms of curation for a discussion. What are your thoughts on format or how you approach each?

Mevis: Books can physically survive over time, but in the case of an digital book, where the book is gone when the devices change, we no longer have access to that information. So I don't think that the device replaces the printed book, but rather, they coexist next to each other. If we gave up making books, we would be making a huge mistake, because we will lose a lot of knowledge.

How do you react to the lifespan of your work, where the audience can make their own version of one of your designs, perhaps not in line with how you perceived it or intended it to be?

Mevis: You can never control that. You know what you do, if it's right or not, or if you succeeded or not, but once you hand it over, it gets its own life. There can be people who don't understand it, who create another story, or who dislike it, but that doesn't affect me anymore.

How much control do you believe you have as a designer and how do you deal with unexpected results?

Mevis: At first, because you know what you want to do, you control the situation, but when the person on the other side of the table doesn't like what you propose, you lose control. That is when it becomes difficult. Sometimes you can find a good solution, still doing something you like and support, but other times you can end up in situations where you just want to finish the work, because there is no way to convince that other person to take the direction you had in mind. But there should always be something in each project that allows you to engage yourself with.

You developed a new visual identity for Chicago's Museum of Contemporary Art (MCA) in

2015. At which moment did you tell the MCA that "from now on, we're no longer part of the game"?

Mevis: When the contract ended; it's the moment that we hand over the work to the client. With the MCA, we would have liked to do one more step into the direction of applications. Luckily, they hired Dylan Fracareta as the design director at the MCA, who was a former student of ours. He came a few times to Amsterdam where we met in a workshop-style situation to work on different hypothetical scenarios.

You stated you wanted to play a more active role in redesigning the institution, including engagement with the building, which is in the realm of architecture. What led you to see the practices of architecture and graphic design as being part of a single solution?

Mevis: When we came to the MCA for the first time, we entered a building that is quite overwhelming in what it is. We immediately expressed a desire to address the spaces. We wanted to put the MCA in a different spotlight, so people would have another experience. So we thought about its architecture, the way the entrance area is organized, where you buy your tickets, and what you see when you enter—aspects which are important in rethinking the identity within the building, and for the people who come to visit. We understood that it's not our profession, but we proposed to them to consider an architectural intervention as well. We asked: how could architecture and graphic design come together? They appreciated our proposals, but also said that it's a different project to rethink the architecture. They are currently working with architects to improve logistics. It will be interesting to see how the architectural and the graphic identity become one integrated project.

>With the MCA or the Stedelijk Museum in
>Amsterdam, how has the leadership at those
>institutions influenced your work, if at all?

Mevis: We were appointed for the Stedelijk project by another director, and everyone who was there when we started as the designers of the new Stedelijk Museum has left by now. In the past two or three years, we've seen a completely new team of people arrive. For them, perhaps we represent something of the past, so there is a huge difference between how we worked under the first director, and under the second director. With the first director, we were constantly in touch, where we could send emails to each other and discuss things, and now we no longer have that kind of access. So in talking about leadership, that's where it slowly starts to affect the work, and make you insecure. When a new team doesn't try to involve you in the same way, preferring to create more distance, is a kind of a critique of you and your work. The museum would benefit from a stronger bond with the designers.

>This leads us back to the question of how the
>rules are defined to a client in terms of the
>work you will produce for them.

Mevis: The strange thing in the world of museums, or maybe art in general, is that when someone new steps in, he or she wants to rearticulate the program. A new director comes in and has another idea about how to articulate that through graphic design. Companies work differently. When you have a brand and a new CEO steps in, they don't change the brand, because they are much more aware that consistency has big value. Museums should realize when they have a strong brand, for instance as the MoMA in New York City does, you should stick more to it. It's not beneficial to completely redesign an identity, if it is strong.

What differences have you encountered when designing the identity of a museum in Europe versus America?

Mevis: In America, it's a much larger undertaking to change an identity—at least that's how I experienced it with the MCA. In our sessions with the Stedelijk, it was a very small committee, and decisions were made in a very informal way, whereas the MCA also involved trustees, making the table bigger and creating a bigger support system. This means that if, for instance, the MCA Director Madeleine Grynsztejn leaves, it doesn't immediately change everything because it was supported by a much bigger team at its inception. That is a key difference between the American situation and the European or Dutch situation, in part because the museums here are privately funded with donations, which gives them a say in what happens.

You stated earlier that you "only work with ten fonts because I can't remember all the others." It is a strength, an act of control, to limit yourself in this manner?

Mevis: It means you don't have to consider the same amount of options as young, beginning designers, because to them everything is still possible. You know there are many places you don't even want to go anymore because you've either seen it or you have no interest in it. So in the area where you want to operate, you can be more precise, and go deeper and become sharper. When I proposed an idea for *Wiel Arets—Bas Princen*, it was not a very exceptional idea, just a very simple idea, but to make it work, you have to stick to it. Because as soon as you start to give it up, there is nothing left anymore. When you bring something small, there is not so much that can be negotiated. As opposed to a situation like the MCA, where it's much richer, meaning more elements, and you have to negotiate about all of them, and you can replace them, or leave them out, or do something completely different, and the identity would still not be harmed. With a simple idea, the moves are limited, which doesn't lessen the decisions but gives you more precise decisions to work with.

DOMINIQUE PERRAULT

You've stated that your interest in architecture is to "introduce new, dialectical situations and experiences," for example between inside and outside, public and private. What is the relationship, for you, between the physical and the cultural?

Perrault: Architecture should be very emotional and visceral even without culture, because architecture is about feeling. Obviously, it's better and much richer when there is a cultural aspect, but I think the first relationship—the first contact with a building—is always physical. One can perceive the light in the corner, the staircase in front of them, or the evident structure. At the beginning it is a totally abstract, mental relationship, but at the end it's physical. The "Kolonihaven" installation in Copenhagen, Denmark, in July 1996, for the Louisiana Museum of Modern Art explains what I believe to be the core of architecture very well. For the project we chose a tree around which to place an intervention of four walls of glass. Condensation appears on the panels of glass in the morning and the walls began disappear as they reflect the nature around them. When you are an architect, it's is very symbolic even to build some walls. You make a statement about the space inside, and the space outside.

Could you comment on the prominence of the architectural void in your projects, starting with the National Library of France [1995]?

Perrault: For me, the main idea of architecture, especially in a large institutional building like the National

Library of France, is about how to manage the presence of the public space or the outside, with the building or the inside. In the conception of the project, I wanted to cultivate a special attitude about the presence of the void, which, for me, is the most interesting material that can be put to use for architecture. The void can create a relationship between the private and the public that is very strong. With the library, the four corners create a boundary around a virtual volume, like a big box, which is sunk underground, below the public space of an esplanade. The void separates the private part of the library, around the garden, from the public part, which is the public plaza for the new district. It also creates a kind of relationship between the natural and the artificial, because we planted this small forest of trees twenty feet below street level. It's totally artificial. It's a huge building, but the high density doesn't even exist at street level, from the perspective from the pedestrian bridge above the Seine River. All you see is a void in the skyline.

> Is context similarly a single material with a general set of properties that can be deployed for architecture, or must it be broken down into its individual components?

Perrault: If you are a romantic, you work with context in an attempt to expand it and protect each part. Yet for a conceptual architect like myself, the context is a type of material. I can touch it, change it, or keep it. But, it does not transform my process. I think the concept of a building can be detached from its context; I don't like to visit the site before I have thought through the concept for the project. If I did, and if the context was beautiful, I would think that it is not necessary to build a building. If the context was awful, I would be disappointed and it would affect the outcome of the project. So it's best if, initially, I work with as little information about the site as possible, perhaps just a photograph, and launch a dialogue after the site visit. So, the context is not always an acute situation that simply provides constraints. I am not respectful of the context like a historicist architect of the nineteenth century, or a contemporary preservationist. I want to immediately change the quality of this context into another context with an even better quality. The power of architecture is to transform the place into another place. I think that is the responsibility of the architect today; if you don't transform, you, in fact, build nothing. By burying a project, or making the architecture otherwise disappear, there is a promotion of a new context.

> Do you believe you managed to achieve such a transformation of context with the Berlin Velodrome and Olympic Swimming Pool [1997; 1999]?

Perrault: For the Velodrome and Swimming Pool in Berlin, Germany, the idea was to utilize the same components as the National Library in Paris—building and nature. We developed a big orchard with apple trees into which we introduced two buildings in the center. The main idea was to create very large buildings that have a special location within the urban fabric, yet are open; there are no fences, grids, or columns to block the public from using this as a public space. This type of building works to open up the space between itself and the space around. In this sense, the project is political. After the 1936 Berlin Olympics, which were organized under the Nazi regime, this project presented a way to secure the buildings for the population, and play up the lack of political or military use. All four sides are open, with this garden to create connections and relationships between different parts of this district. This type of public space is open territory, and for me, it also relates to ideas present in the modern movement. Here we see the possibility to

DOMINIQUE PERRAULT ARCHITECTURE,
"KOLONIHAVEN" INSTALLATION, COPENHAGEN,
DENMARK, 1996. GLASS PANELS THAT BEGIN TO
DISAPPEAR AS CONDENSATION FORMS ON THEM
IN THE EARLY MORNING.

introduce more density into the city, again, without the presence of a lot of buildings.

> Are you able to build on the existing presence of nature in the metropolis, such as parks or water features, in your quest to negate the architecture?

Perrault: It's possible to develop this kind of strategy with, for example, our Conference Center in Saint-Germain-en-Laye, France, in 1991. It's a park with a manor in the center that we did on the west part of Paris. The idea was to transform this existing building into a small conference center. We introduced a glass disc, like a pool, around the manor, and this pool covers the auditorium and underground cafe below. With this small void, we created the artificial presence of water in the park. We kept the presence of nature, and we changed the quality of the architecture of this manor. The manor was not a beautiful building, but the interest in this building is about its existing condition. And this existing condition is, for me, a route to develop a project from this material, the existing condition. We used the same strategy for the Dobrée Museum in the center of the city of Nantes, France, which won an international competition in 2010. We were near a garden with different buildings, and the idea was to develop a connection between these three buildings, one from the seventeenth century, one from the fifteenth, and one from the nineteenth century. We proposed to build a new building just behind the building of the nineteenth century, on a new space. And I proposed not to build vertically, the building, but to build horizontally, the new building, and connect with a temporary gallery, with a foyer, with a main entrance, we are connecting three buildings, and transforming these three buildings into one museum. When we organized the pedestrian path around the museum, and we kept the garden, and created a special mirror with a water film, patio space, and green roofs, and merged these different components to create a very special and specific garden around the building.

Our current focus at IIT is "Rethinking Metropolis." What is your position on this issue?
Perrault: Research and practice are the same, not only in my office but in my mind as well. There is no difference. The client, the political, economic, social situation, and existing condition—these are all materials in a process. It's a very objective and clear way to develop research. For me, the metropolis is not a city, the metropolis is a substance. It is comprised of different cities existing within different landscapes and infrastructure. It is a new urban structure, and I think we should try to work out what it is by focusing on the specificity of the metropolis. For example, a lot of architects in the Atelier International du Grand Paris (AIGP), a laboratory of applied ideas of which I was a member of the scientific council and representative of a multidisciplinary team, do work on the huge territory of greater Paris. They have some interesting ideas, good designs, and a lot of imagination, but they approach the problems from the perspective of the global to local. It's clear to me that it should be done in the opposite way. With social networks and other mapping technologies, we have the ability to extract the global from millions of data points at our disposal. This gives us the ability to explain the specificity of the network and work on designing for localized populations. The Grand Paris social network is more or less 12 million inhabitants. My belief is that ten percent of these inhabitants are new inhabitants. A recent arrival in Paris might try to develop networks, and an economy emerges around them, such as co-working, and apartment or bike sharing. This creates an interesting situation in which to intervene for researchers and designers.

> How does the architectural research impact
> the requirements of design in this instance?

It was part of a case study in 2013 for the AIGP, called Living in Greater Paris. If this huge territory has a diameter of around 60 kilometers, and you are seventy years of age, you are 40 kilometers from a good hospital. You spend a lot of time on the metro and life becomes impossible. To get past this problem we proposed organizing, within specific populations such as young students, older retirees, middle aged couples, and so on, special points—a device we called "Hotel Metropole." It was like a Swiss Army knife of 500,000 to one million square-meters with hybrid functions. These special points of hybrid function could adapt to new programs to provide the growing city with multiple points of interaction for its occupants, and provide places within the city to stay for a couple of days when one has to travel across it. We have a need for this kind of urban program and building in the metropole because the metropole is very aggressive. A lot of stress is being placed on our public transportation systems. In a way it's like a body. If you abuse it too much, the metropolis becomes tired. This type of research and thinking is crucial to design today, as a successful metropolis always reflects the high quality of humanity within it.

> We like your idea of meta-buildings that fill a
> void in the present social order of cities. How-
> ever, very few buildings around the world even
> come close to the scale that you've mentioned.
> Why do you think it is so difficult to realize
> projects this large?

Perrault: The scale of these buildings is not the problem. I have no problem with the scale. I think scale exists only in relation to context, where there is a very strong and efficient relationship between the object and the context. Working with territory that large and wide, the scale of

DOMINIQUE PERRAULT ARCHITECTURE, EWHA
WOMANS UNIVERSITY, SEOUL, SOUTH KOREA,
2008. VIEW OF THE "STREET" BETWEEN TWO
WALLS.

the building and the scale of the context should evolve together so that they work together. You can immediately change the quality of the context by what you put in it. Take the Pinault Foundation of Contemporary Art in Boulogne-Billancourt, France, an international invited competition we participated in for the Renault site in 2001, where, instead of building a building, we built a landscape. In a sense, we rebuilt the memory of this island. The site had once been a very famous factory in Paris for Renault, and this factory had changed; buildings had disappeared or were even destroyed. We imagined wrapping the site with a metal fabric or mesh that would designate the different functions of a museum. Each function was a box, and by installing boxes stacked on top of one another, the space between the walls and the mesh fabric became the in-between and specialized spaces. The mesh acted like a tissue through which the inside of the buildings and the outside or public space was blurred. The geometric volumes disappear underneath this metal fabric and work as if they are the same surface of a small mountain, or small hill; they are a landscape. This, in turn, definitively changed the functional status of the architecture and its context.

> So, would you think of a meta-building as a civic building that distills the programmatic elements of the city into a compact form that has a wider effect in the metropolis?

Perrault: It's a matter of the design concept, which provides the presence of the building. The power of the architect is the control the presence of the architecture. Between [Charles] de Gaulle in the 1950s, the Grand Projets of [Francois] Mitterrand in the 1980s, and now, we have totally lost the vision to develop French territory. We have created some new cities, but there is no connection between these cities and projects. The Grand-Projets, as an urban planning project, have been a historical mistake. As a result, now we are trying to develop new connections with metros, but for me, it is evidence of a clear reaction, a psychological reaction of the French people, against the modern project. The focus of the design needs to be placed on the connection between the projects, and how they are considered democratically.

> Kenneth Frampton talks about Hannah Arendt and her term, "the space of public appearance." What sort of spaces do you imagine these to be? For example in Paris, there are some public spaces like old parks that work like extensions of the living room, but on the other hand, there are spaces like Le Cent Quatre that are intended to be spontaneous, collaborative spaces.

Perrault: At the moment, Paris is not so spontaneous because of the public space it has maintained for centuries. The nice avenues with very good urban design are only accessible for the rich people. They are the people who don't drink in the basement bars. The relationship between the population of Paris is a very aggressive one. The people living in the building and the people using the ground floor of the city do not necessarily have the same idea of that space. If you ask me what sort of spaces should be imagined, the evidence points to an increase in the depth of the ground levels of a lot of buildings. It's what I propose in *Groundscapes: Other Topographies* [Éditions HYX, 2016], my recent monograph focusing on the concept of underground architecture that I've been exploring and experimenting with since the 1980s. The ground level of a lot of buildings are very nice because of the high volume of people, however with small roads and buildings overall, it is not efficient for the people living and working there. Parisian public space was designed during the nineteenth century as a two-dimensional design. It is very old fashioned and it follows a narrative and figurative design. We now design in three dimensions so why not take advantage of that.

> If we now look to Chicago, what can we learn from Paris, and what do you see as new potentials in the development of the city and its architecture?

Perrault: For me, the question is not about Chicago. For me, Chicago is the most beautiful city in the United States, because it's an American city with a design or presence like a European city. New York City has a special culture, but it is in a different lineage category. And so I would say I have two points to answer such a question. The first, would be that in the United States, the relationship between the city and the public space is not clear. Step by step, the public clients in Chicago have understood the importance and the value of public space. Because of the relationship with the lake that Chicago has, the question about public space concerns the infrastructure that establishes barriers between the city and its beautiful lake. There should be a strategic plane that reconnects or develops new links between the lake and the city. It's fantastic to have the presence of this natural element so close to all the very elegant architecture, but the American people have not evaluated the public space they have. Public space in America today is not contemporary. It does not work to combine the private and the public situation for something other than money.

> Since 2013, you are Professor at the Ecole Polytechnique Fédérale de Lausanne (EPFL), Switzerland, and Director of the research laboratory for Underground Architecture (SUB). What are the new emerging generation of architects working on there?

DOMINIQUE PERRAULT ARCHITECTURE,
NATIONAL LIBRARY OF FRANCE, PARIS, FRANCE,
1995. VIEW OF GARDEN BELOW GROUND.

Perrault: I think in Lausanne, the vision, or perhaps the ideology, of the school is like a triangle between the architectural field, the biological field, and the engineering field. It is a polytechnic school after all. However, what is interesting is that we have the goal to coordinate these three fields and work together. For example, for my theme "underground," I am working together with a Swiss woman, who has worked with the pathology of light, and a male Chinese engineer who has done research on the underground city. We are constantly trying to coordinate exchanges between the themes of architecture, biology, and engineering. It's not easy due to the distance, but I think it's a new form of practice. Especially for students, it's an interesting opportunity to have contact with other territories.

> A final question on the role of the underground and it's usage in the future. How do you see public architecture moving forward with your proposals for using more of the underground?

Perrault: It is most evident in my statement about my intent to build a landscape and not a building for the Ewha Womans University, Seoul, South Korea, in 2008. It was a women's university that began as an American missionary 125 years ago. Now, this school has become a very important university in Asia. However, the problem with the campus was the connection between the campus territory and the city. Twenty years ago, the territory was totally closed to the city. The staff of the university thus organized an architectural competition to install a new entrance and connection between the territory of the campus and the district. My idea was not a new building or new pavilions, but to develop a landscape that connected with the existing landscape as an expansion from the metro station. Hence the idea was to organize the campus into a street—one between two walls, like a valley in the center of a hill. The new entrance followed the same route that the students took when coming onto the campus, but beneficially introduced into this route a new underground landscape, that contained buildings. This was a very friendly, sensual, and emotional relationship between the existing condition and the high density of the Asian city. This kind of architecture is always very impressive, because you can walk through architecture without feeling its presence. This type of solution is a good answer to several urban situations. It's not unique, and it's not the unique answer, but, it does represent the very good connection between the underground layer of facilities and ground layer of the street and urban space. This relationship is so often lost as the connection between the two isn't often expressed. And I think it's certainly a solution to the development of a contemporary architecture with new feelings, new kinds of comfort, and new facilities.

It is my opinion that the modern movement, especially Le Corbusier, did not want to touch the ground floor. Being the puritan he was, he did not want to touch the soil. Such a puritan relationship between architecture and its ground floor limited the thinking of the modern movement. And it is not until now that contemporary architecture is looking at it. Geography is now one of the most important parts in the process of an architect; to think, to speak, and to feel the architecture. The underground presents an opportunity for a totally different world. Now, the planet has all but been completely discovered. We now know what is happening on every inch of the earth, and so we must ask ourselves, where is the future? It is in a new approach to the difference between the artificial and the natural on the planet and in the city. And for me, the underground presents a very rich and special layer to develop another kind of comfort, and quality for architecture; especially on an urban scale. A lot of commissions are arriving now that aim to restore, and to change existing buildings into another building with another function. It is a big market for architecture, and for the architect it presents the opportunity to make use of the existing conditions while finding new realms of contemporary living that will suffice into the future.

STAN ALLEN

You work simultaneously as a theorist, educator, and practitioner of architecture. How do these three roles intersect in a productive way for you and your practice?

Allen: For me, they're all different aspects of what it means to be an architect. But there are important differences in the techniques involved. Writing is a practice that has its own rules and techniques—you have to respect those rules and work within the limits of those techniques. The mistake comes when you confuse discursive practices such as writing with a material practice such as design. So it's not a question of theory versus practice; they're parallel practices. The third aspect, education, is simply a way to continue the discussion around architecture by sharing that knowledge and passing it on to another generation. Obviously, there are practical struggles: sometimes you get pulled in many directions, but they are all complimentary practices and it would be hard for me to imagine taking any one of the three out of the equation.

But does one have a stronger impact than the other two?

Allen: In my case, practice drives the other two. I write from the perspective of a practicing architect and I teach from the perspective of a practicing architect.

Do you think all architects should be writing or teaching?

Allen: Not necessarily. I don't think you can be an effective architect without a self-critical distance and a reflection on your practice, but it doesn't mean that all architects have to sit down and produce articles. That self-reflection can take many forms—exhibitions, lectures, teaching. Lately, when people ask me why I've been writing less, I point out that I write a lot in practice. The ability to express yourself in written and verbal form is a big part of practice today.

What do you believe is the most relevant contemporary theory on urbanism today?

Allen: In the twentieth century, under both modernism and post-modernism, the big issues were all linked to technological change: first with mechanized technology and later with digital technology. I believe that today, the big issues of the twenty-first century will have to do with man's relationship to nature. And nature—which was once excluded from the city, or only allowed in under highly specific conditions such as parklands—is now re-occupying the city. As we think about urbanism, we have to identify the ways in which this fundamentally new relationship between nature and the city—which extends all the way from climate change to the biotic ecologies of the body—will impact the metropolis. We haven't really considered this at a deeper level.

You've written on this topic in the past. Do you think that your previous writings are as relevant today, in this time of continuous, rapid change?

Allen: It depends on how far back you go. You get to a point in your career where you can step back from things you wrote twenty-five years ago and see that the issues you were talking about, and even the way you were writing, were marked by the time period. On the other hand, with regards to some of the theory/practice debates, I realize my position hasn't changed very much since the 1990s. I hope that the writing has gotten a little clearer over time, but I think it goes back to your first question. Because I'm not a scholar or historian, I'm really writing to work out issues that have an impact on my practice. I mean, we could go through specific articles and I could say what is and isn't still relevant but "Infrastructural Urbanism," which I wrote in the 1990s, is still relevant, but today I would overlay that with ideas of ecology and adaptation. "Field Conditions" is another piece that I wrote in the mid-1990s that keeps coming back and still has an impact on my work today. So I think there's been a lot of continuity, along with some new themes that have been introduced.

> Earlier in your career, you had the opportunity to work with James Corner of Field Operations. Are large-scale urban landscaping projects still a concern of yours? It seems as if you are redirecting your attention in your work.

Allen: I collaborated with Jim Corner for three years, from 1999-2003, during which time we did the Downsview Competition in Toronto, and Fresh Kills in New York City. I learned a lot from that experience, but it's now quite a while ago, and you are correct to say that I am slowly moving away from that kind of work. There are a number of reasons, some of which are quite trivial: a lot of that work is located far from New York City and I'm also impatient with the very, very long timeline of implementation. We recently did the masterplan for the reuse of the Metropolitan Airport in Taichung, Taiwan. It was accepted three years ago but it's probably going to be twenty years before it's built. I just don't have the patience to see a big complicated project like that through for the next twenty years of my life. So although I believe the ideas of landscape urbanism are extremely import-

STAN ALLEN, TAICHUNG INFOBOX, TAICHUNG,
TAIWAN, 2011. VIEW OF BAMBOO SCAFFOLDING.

ant, and the field can continue to learn from the realities of implementation, it's partly due to institutional frustration that I'm less interested in it today. So that's the logistical side. The second thing is that despite the theoretical promise, I think we need to be critical of landscape urbanism for staying too much within the disciplinary expertise of landscape architecture. Landscape urbanists by and large, are not actually doing urbanism, they're doing landscape architecture. Julia Czerniak, in her recent book Large Parks, got it right: people who claim to be practicing landscape urbanism today are basically doing landscape architecture on a very large scale. Instead, our conceptual framework should be: "Can we learn from landscape but recover the disciplinary agency of architecture, even within a freestanding object-building?" The interdisciplinary aspects of landscape urbanism were very exciting to me, but I was not on board with that project if it meant redefining myself as a landscape architect. The third thing I want to say is that the larger issues that interested me about landscape urbanism, namely the relationship to nature and ecology, can also operate in very small-scale projects. You don't necessarily have to be working at a very large scale to be dealing with questions of nature and ecology.

> To expand on that last point, you wrote that, "Landform building is less interested in the imitation of natural form and more interested in new programmatic possibilities that are opened up by the creation of artificial terrains." Yet in your lectures you mostly describe the morphological (formal) organizational structures and focus less on the programmatic opportunities. Could you comment on that?

Allen: I did write that, so I can't disown the statement. Going back to the 1990s, when architects first rediscovered landscape, I think it offered architecture three really important possibilities. First, a model of smooth connectivity. This was also when early computer software emerged, enabling surface modeling and the idea that you could make connections through warped and folded surfaces. Landscape offered a great model for connectivity accomplished through surfaces. The second thing was indeterminate programming. Landscape programming is different from architectural programming. Architectural programming has antecedents in functionalism, and is very much about mapping functions onto particular spaces, whereas when you think about a public park and the potential activities that can happen within a landscape, there's an open-ended envelope of programs. Landscape offers a model of directed space that is open and flexible with regard to program. The third thing that landscape offered architects was a model for change over time. So your question relates to the second of those three opportunities, but it's impossible to talk about program without connecting it to form. In my recent work, I continue to be interested in what we used to refer to as "loose fit," back at Columbia in the 1990s. The loose fit between program and activity; the idea that, as opposed to the one-to-one mapping of functionalism, there is a loose envelope of program that can happen within any given space, which is in turn, is specific to a formal configuration. I'm suspicious of the notion that architects script program. I think what we do is lay out a field of possibilities and then it's really up to citizens to collectively and creatively activate the space. As a democratic or political model, it's the public that has to exercise their freedom of choice. It's not something to be dictated by an architect.

Could you give a specific example where you're directing the functions of the space in one of your projects?

Allen: The first projects I ever built as an architect were art galleries. And it involved an old debate: "How much does the architecture of the exhibition space influence the viewing of the work, and how intrusive should the architecture be? Should it just be the so-called neutral white box or can the architecture be more active?" It became a question of how you navigate that tension, because the gallery is a space that is not complete until it is occupied by the artworks. Someone other than the architect responds to the space, an artist or a gallery director with a curatorial vision. The architect doesn't do that. So my job was to create a kind of infrastructure or platform for somebody else to come in and react to what I was doing, and create the final definition of the space. I think I hold onto that idea in many different scales, from museum projects we've done to some of the smaller single family houses. As an architect, I create a kind of framework that will steer and direct the activities of the people who use the space without over-determining and dictating what happens within that space.

> If function emerges from the forms that you design, how do you gauge the effectiveness of your decisions, or the performance of the forms before they are realized?

Allen: I have a counterintuitive approach to this. Engineers design to performance specifications, and if a highway or a bridge doesn't meet those specifications, it fails. I believe architecture fails not-by-not arriving at its performance specifications but rather, by foreclosing future possibilities, that is to say, by a too narrow definition of function that doesn't allow for the unexpected. A successful piece of architecture is one where something happens that was not originally anticipated by the architect.

In your book, *Landform Building* [Lars Müller Publishers, 2011], you identified this type as a growing trend in recent architectural projects. What are the societal factors that have contributed to this trend?

Allen: Landform building is interesting to me because it's a symptom of the larger cultural phenomenon—a preoccupation with the question of the relationship between man and nature, which is also consistent with the current discourse on environmental sustainability. With the book, I hoped to do two things simultaneously: one was simply document a trend, but the other was to be somewhat critical toward that trend. Specifically, I'm critical of what I call the "softly-rounded mound" strategy. This is the vulnerable cliché of landform building, and it arises out of a false integration of nature and architecture. I'm against the idea that you can just make buildings literally continuous with the landscape, or imitate the forms of landscape. There are very few examples of that being done successfully. It's too much of a camouflage strategy, where you're simply covering over the boundary between nature and culture. Again, it's something we want to document and pay attention to, but to also look at with a certain degree of skepticism. The value of the book was to present a series of compelling projects that go beyond the cliché of the landform.

You often describe the organization of your work with verbs, such as the index you developed for *Landform Building*. Most of your work contains an embedded component of time.

Allen: Yes.

So how does something like a building, which is usually unchanging, become an entity that acts?

Allen: You're absolutely correct and this is the fallacy of animate form. Buildings are in fact static by nature and so it's helpful to think of architecture not as biological (animate, or literally moving), but as more of a geological entity. I like the distinction Manuel De Landa lays out in *A Thousand Years of Nonlinear History* [Zone Books, 1997] between the linguistic, the biological, and the geological. Architecture in the last twenty-five years has focused on the linguistic and biological, whereas I think it's more geological by nature—it's hard, durable and slow. In other words, it's more mineral than it is animal or vegetable. It's correct to identify architecture as an entity that is fundamentally static, but you have to understand that in the context of ecological theory, which looks at the interplay between the organism and it's environment. What ecological theories tell us is that it's never a relationship between a stable ground and actively changing organisms, but rather that they both are always interacting with one another, and co-evolving. The difference between geology and biology in this instance is that geological formations also change, they just change very slowly. You can say the same thing about architecture. Architecture moves and changes, it just moves and changes very slowly. By saying yes, architecture is identified with the mineral and geological, which is more stable, yet it has a complex interaction with organisms or animate life, we learn that it's in the interrelationship that things happen. So architecture is not necessarily the entity that acts, it's the users and inhabitants who act, but they act in response to the conditions that architecture imposes. For many years, architecture was identified as a fixed and stable ground, then the pendulum swung in the opposite direction, we had computer software that make things spin and move, and we got very excited about animate form. I think we went a little too far in the opposite direction. So in some sense for me it's a corrective to stress architecture's mineral,

STAN ALLEN, SALIM PUBLISHING HOUSE, PAJU
BOOK CITY, KOREA, 2009. EXTERIOR VIEW.

geological character, while being careful to say that even mineral matter is vibrant and active and capable of changing over time.

> On the other hand, you describe practices as dynamic, unfolding in time, and having trajectories. Do you see your office as having a trajectory and if so, could you describe what that trajectory is?

Allen: Yes, there is a long trajectory. In general terms, it's been a trajectory from very small-scale works to an engagement in the city, and then scaling up to regional ecologies and landscape. Now my interest is in bringing that back down in scale, and taking some of the lessons from landscape and ecology and thinking about how can they operate in smaller-scale projects. I admit there's a logistical and practical side to this—being able to work on projects that are closer to home where you can see them going up and you can be more closely involved in the process. You see this trajectory in a lot of offices: they start small, they get big, and many people are interested in bigness but it's not necessary that the trajectory of a practice or office must end there. I think it's important for an architect to work on projects at different scales, not only because they work on different issues at different scales, but also because they involve different time frames and speeds. A big urban project may have a five or six-year horizon of implementation, whereas a small house you can see built in a year. Over time the lessons of the larger-scale work find their way into the smaller-scale work, and vice-versa.

> What is the most important disciplinary discussion that we as architects should be having today?

Allen: The fundamental question that we have to resolve in the next few decades is our relationship to the planet. By that, I don't mean architecture is going to save the planet, because I don't believe it can. It's true that buildings are responsible for approximately 40 percent of our carbon footprint and it would be irresponsible for us as architects to ignore the new potentials available to us to build in a less harmful way. Just as it's irresponsible to make a building that would fall down, it's irresponsible to make a building that consumes an excessive amount of energy. But I don't think you get points for that. That's basic, good professional practice, and responsible citizenship. The discourse around sustainability is a bit like the war on drugs—it's a battle that's never going to be won. The numbers just don't add up. 85–90 percent of the environment is already built, so if you were to build the remaining 10 percent, even at a replacement rate of 2–3 percent per year, and you built it 50 percent more sustainably, you're still not going to make a dent in the problem. So, making any kind of significant impact on global warming and climate change is not going to come from architectural practice. It's going to come from much larger changes in society. As architects, in our capacity as cultural workers expanding the horizon of imagination, I think we can give people models about different ways to live which may in turn have a larger impact on lifestyles and the way cities are built. But we're not going to save the planet by implementing the standards of LEED.

The Cloud Studio here at IIT engages in research-based design. I'm curious if traditional research or data plays any role in your studio.
Allen: It doesn't. David Shapiro, a poet who taught at Cooper Union, liked to repeat a line from Roman Jakobson who was in turn quoting Aleksandr Pushkin, and he said, "Measurements are good, as we know, for pota-

toes." I'm not a data guy but because I have a lot of respect for the hard scientists, I know that data has to be used in a very rigorous way. I don't think architects use data in a very rigorous way; we tend to marshal data to support an argument. I just don't think we're very good researchers. Access to data is not a problem today—in fact we have too much data; the real issue is to understand what counts among all the data that inundates us daily—that's a creative and critical function. We can have a much greater impact by showing people new forms of social organization and new potential ways of living than by marshaling ever greater numbers of data. It's also a fallacy to think that data is going to lead you to a solution. The data will might show you what the problem is, but there's still a need for creativity to come up with a response. Architecture is a creative practice. It's not a research profession or a research science.

> Another thing we do here is "progressive research." That is, speculating about the city, conditions, sites, building types, and lifestyles in the future. Do you have a position on the metropolis of the future?

Allen: I can get onboard with "progressive research." It's speculative. Architecture is a projective discipline, making propositions about an unknown future. Fortunately, we're not scientists who have to back up our hypothesis with data, we just make up propositions about the future. Again, we do have to act responsibly not to over-determine that future, and leave room for other political actors and political subjects to find their own way within that. Perhaps I can modify my statement from earlier: I think that the most important issue that we have to deal with is the relationship between man and nature in the future. The territory on which that relationship is going to play out is the realm of global urbanism. In 2008 we passed the threshold where more than 50 percent of the global population now lives in urbanized areas. It's projected to something like 75 percent by mid-century and the majority of those cities are in developing countries. Those are the places where the new conditions, sites, types, and lifestyles are playing out most urgently and those are the areas that the profession needs to focus on in the next twenty to fifty years.

> Do you have any advice for us on how to begin engaging those areas?

Allen: I think architects and architectural students have become very good at recognizing where the important issues are today. Where I think we are all lagging behind is identifying the techniques to intervene effectively within those systems and to mobilize the agency of architecture to really have an impact. That in and of itself requires creativity, flexibility, and inventing new tools of representation and design. I think you have to ask yourself continually, "How could architecture make a difference within this situation?" Or to use the famous phrase from Gregory Bateson, "What are the differences that make a difference?" In other words, what variable could architecture effect within the system that would cause a larger scale change? The answer isn't always obvious and doesn't always default to something that's been done in the past.

> In a past interview with Luca Farinelli of Log, when you were asked "Corb or Mies?" you said "Corb." Why?

Allen: I know, I know. Are you familiar with Isaiah Berlin's famous distinction between the hedgehog and the fox? He was talking about writers and intellectuals, and he said that there are hedgehogs who have one big issue and they work deliberately and consistently and, as they move forward, they develop a very singular point of view and they don't deviate from it. And then there are foxes that jump around, touching on this or that. They move from issue to issue, question to question. I think his simple description is that the hedgehog knows one big thing, and the fox knows many little things. Mies was a hedgehog, and Corb was a fox. I think that's pretty clear. I think in terms of my own sensibility I am more a fox and less of a hedgehog. It's not necessarily a value judgment, they're just different artistic, creative, and intellectual styles.

Are any hedgehogs still left in the profession? Allen: That's a great question. Yes, I think you could safely say the hedgehog is an endangered species, and not just in architecture. We live in a time where agility and the ability to change and adapt is more important, so I think we do tend to value foxes more than hedgehogs today. Maybe we need more hedgehogs, I don't know. Perhaps we need more dinosaurs. Now I'm going to get in trouble because people will think I said Mies is a dinosaur. He's not.

BERNARD KHOURY

On returning to post-civil war Beirut in 1993, your early works reflected your belief that "the country was in a period of great hope of reconstruction." Do you still think this romanticism was the right approach?

Khoury: That was a trap many of us fell into during the early 1990s. It was only natural for those in my generation, in the creative fields, to try and address questions that had to do with memory and our recent past, as a reaction to postwar amnesia. My first built works were an obvious attempt to do that.

If your first built work is an entertainment destination, on what used to be a refugee camp that burned down to the ground twenty years before, you can either turn your back and walk away, refusing that commission, or you can face the very difficult realities of the site.

The western press were strangely curious about Beirut. Any story on Beirut revolved around this notion of the phoenix rising from the ashes, mythical nonsense that we've been told about Beirut again and again. Also, there were these sugar-coated stories about the glorious past of Beirut—the Switzerland or the Paris of the Middle East, the land where east meets west—which were then suddenly interrupted by another exotic story where we go mad, and the war erupts, as if it were a malady. Then, through a dangerous simplification of history, the war supposedly ends in 1990, which leads to the story of Beirut's former city center rising out of the ashes, and where I am cast as a "bad boy dancing on graves." The story was easy to sell. And that is how I first became visible as an architect. I rode the wave of publicity until I realized that I had become trapped in this narrative.

How has your position evolved over the last twenty years, from this initial stance?

Khoury: I realized years later that dealing with war and violence was a *passage obligé* [obligatory passage] for most artists of my generation, who tried to formulate histories of this territory. Over the last few years, I have been more interested in the mechanisms of survival that were developed on my territory. These also deal with the sour realities that come with working exclusively for the private sector, the bankruptcy of the state and its institutions, and the corruption of the various administrations. For example, most of the volume of building lately was produced for real estate developers. Working closely with them and trying to manipulate, subvert, and hopefully reinvent the prevailing typologies that had been imposed over the last decades, should be considered as an attempt to act not only on the urban fabric, but also on the social fabric.

How do you see the reconstruction of Beirut? Have you ever done a project about it?

Khoury: I often start my lectures with a project that I produced as a student of Lebbeus Woods back in 1991. That was the only studio he ever taught at the [Harvard] GSD. I spent three months with Lebbeus while he was working on *Zagreb Free Zone*, 1991. Until that point, I had never worked on Beirut. I remember that I did not produce a single drawing while with him for over two months as we spent most of our meetings exchanging ideas verbally. Lebbeus was aware of my resistance to aestheticizing war and violence. After these endless conversations, he came to the conclusion that I did not need to design a project like the others in the group. He felt that our conversations were enough and he exempted me from the expected deliverables of the design studio. In the two weeks that were left before the final pin-up, I produced Evolving Scars, a project that he saw for the first time with the other members of the jury at the final crit. They included Michael Sorkin, Hani Rashid, and other friends of his. That specific project tackled the demolition of many condemned buildings right at the beginning of the so-called reconstruction of the Beirut historical city center. I still consider it an important exercise, as it turned the process of demolition into an architectural act. This goes against the very nature of our practice, which consists of erecting matter. On a more political level, Evolving Scars dealt with issues of memory of our recent past. For me, there could be no reconstruction before the scars inflicted by our recent conflict were healed. Lebbeus defended me fiercely, and this was the beginning of a long friendship. He was a great educator, probably the best I have had throughout my academic years.

> How do you see the role of academia in architecture as different from practice?

Khoury: I spent seven years in academic cocoons; five years at RISD [Rhode Island School of Design], followed by two years at GSD and that was enough for me as I felt that the comfort of the academic cocoon can sometimes be dangerous. Spending too much time in academia can disconnect you. There is a huge gap between the difficult realities of the world we are supposed to navigate and what we are prepared to face at school. On another level, I recall getting out of Harvard and not being worth $30,000 a year, compared to friends who had three years of college education who were practicing in

BERNARD KHOURY/DW5, B-018 NIGHTCLUB,
BEIRUT, LEBANON, 1998. VIEW OF OPEN ROOF/
GROUND FAÇADE.

the finance world and were worth four to five times that amount. Not to say that money is all important, but it is a fact that one must take into consideration. While I had a mechanic's hands and had a hard time paying my rent, my friends in finance had perfectly manicured fingers, were well-fed, and drove exotic cars. To further illustrate the bankruptcy of our practice today: an architect cannot build a hotel that has more than twenty keys without a hotel consultant, cannot build a hospital without a hospital consultant, cannot build an airport without an air traffic and airport consultant, and so on. Basically, the manipulation of the architectural program is no longer in our hands. What we are left to work with is the surface and not the substance, while the guardians of our discipline are still safeguarding the good old virtues that define, in their eyes, architecture. But there is nothing left, and it is about time the academic world reconsiders where we stand. I feel that the fate of our practice is in fact quite sad. I refuse to consider architecture an autonomous practice, disconnected from the realities that shape our world. I have a problem with what the academic world produces. In fact, I have a problem with theory, as it tends to generate consensual definitions, which I am not interested in. I have an obsession with the specific.

> You describe your first sixteen projects as "aborted" or unrealized; what was the value of paper architecture for your own career?

Khoury: I don't regret any of them. You have to get in the ring and get beat up to be a good fighter, and I don't think you can win any serious match if you've never been beaten up, ending up on the floor, many times. I got sixteen knock-outs before I scored my first win. That's how I see it.

> Did you carry any of the ideas through to your built work?

Khoury: I wouldn't look at them as specific ideas to be recuperated in projects, but I certainly don't regret the experience. I would like to think that every single project that came after is a very specific situation that requires a very specific strategy, and a very specific answer.

> Reflecting on your built work, how does your connection to the past affect how you build for the future?

Khoury: To answer relative to my practice, keep in mind that everything I do is for the private sector, and since I'm not very good friends with theory, I work with very specific situations, and very specific conditions that are not so ideal. Through these sometimes extremely difficult and sour conditions, we try to produce meaning. This brings us to the present, where we're so grounded that we don't have time to romanticize the past nor speculate about the future in theoretical terms. We revisit the past only through the eyes of the present and let the future take care of itself.

> Though you say that your work is highly contextual, you also aim to inject an "instrument of pleasure" into place? The Club B018, for instance, sits on ground that could have been appropriate as a war memorial.

Khoury: The first six projects I built were temporary projects, on grounds that were under convalescence. They had an expiration date before I even designed them. That club you're referring to, B018, is on a problematic site that could have been the site of a memorial for the war if we were in a nation that could have rebuilt itself. Beirut was never rebuilt, because we never agreed on a shared history. With that, the notion of the nation-state was in agony. I do not build monuments and I probably never will. Monuments are the product of an institutional agenda or mission. Where I operate, this is not possible due to the absence, incompetence, bankruptcy, and corruption of our so-called national institutions. As I recognize those sad realities, I still claim that I am one of those hopeless romantics who believe that it is possible, through our practice, to revive or inject energy into areas that are in convalescence. The zone in which the B018 club is located seems to be doomed. Everything around it stinks; that includes the tanneries, the slaughterhouses, the city's garbage collecting company's main facility, army barracks, and my office. The area used to house a refugee camp that was burned down and deserted in 1976. We relocated our design studio there back in 2004, and as we often work late at night, I often hear the sound of the bass beating out of that hole at around four or five in the morning. That's fantastic! On this little plot, where we built our club, we were able to inject energy and pleasure. This, to me, is far more important than what a memorial can do. Memorials provoke contemplative experiences; I prefer to see my projects as devices that are manipulated and abused.

> Quite often while explaining your projects, you talk about forms of resistance. An example is your first built project, which you claim is a battle against the building industry. How do you exercise resistance through architecture?

Khoury: Resistance comes in many different forms, as you have stated. In my early projects, there was an obvious resistance against the standards of the building industry, which I still practice today. It becomes more difficult when you hit larger scales because there are certain mechanisms at work, making it more difficult

BERNARD KHOURY IN COLLABORATION WITH
YASMINE ALMANCHNOUK, DERAILING BEIRUT
INSTALLATION, ROME, ITALY, 2010.

to experiment. But, when you are building 300–400 square-meters for a temporary project, you can afford to carry out these kinds of experiments. The resistance comes through building alliances with people outside the building industry who can make things happen that your basic contractors will not do. To give you an example, no contractor was ready to build the roof of this nightclub, which cost $57,000 at the time. This means I had to look outside the construction industry. I was fortunate enough to meet a magician of a mechanic-welder who had worked for a coach builder on the manufacturing of garbage trucks. My demands, which were impossible to execute through the conventional channels of the construction industry, were in fact relatively simple for that particular artisan. The roof we built together, supposed to last only five years, is now almost eighteen years old. It is opened and closed several times a day, and it has never leaked a single drop of water. As the building survived much longer than what was initially planned, its metal roof structure is now totally rusted. The metal sheets were so thick and heavy that they withstood the test of time, whereas the only water leak resulted from the failure of the waterproofing membrane used in the foundation walls, which was executed by a contractor according to the standards of the construction industry. I still invest great effort in attempting to involve local artisans in the construction of my projects. I learned a lot from this endangered breed of makers, while the rest of the world was abiding by the global standards of the industry. I am also very suspicious of the "green" dictatorship that comes at us in various forms, such as the American LEED or the British BREAM standards. On that front, I often look back, with much greater respect, at the more contextual modes of construction that our fathers employed. Those were in fact far more in tune with not only our climate, but also our social fabric.

Over the last few years, we also fought important battles against the prevailing typologies that were imposed on us by developers. Those consisted of deep slabs, with poorly ventilation, and blind circulation cores located in the center of the plan and landings where you have to turn on the lights in late summerat noon in order to put your key in the door. Those dwellings were conceived to seal the interior inhabitable spaces from their surroundings as much as possible, making the outside seem like hostile territory. They resulted not only bad urban tissue, but also bad social fabric. As a Mediterranean inhabitant, I find that completely unacceptable. The projects we produced in opposition to these standards were, in my opinion, another form of cultural or political resistance.

> From your descriptions we understand Beirut as a radical city of juxtaposition. Where does this radicality lie?

Khoury: Beirut is a city that allows me to contradict myself from one street corner to the next, something I would not be able to do in a more stable environment. Beirut can force you to believe one thing, and its opposite simultaneously. It can also lead you into acrobatic postures in an attempt to develop mechanisms of survival.

> How do you reconcile the spectacle with the "anti-denial" position you claim to take regarding class alienation?

Khoury: In postwar situations, many would often avoid problematic questions by tucking them under the carpet. Others believed that a more meaningful strategy would consist of materializing the sour realities of their context. I find pleasure in manipulating those realities by means of perverting them, sublimating them, and exploring their limits to their fullest extent, in the hope of producing relevant meaning. Sometimes pushing the train beyond its reasonable capacity can lead it to derail, and therefore produce a meaningful accident.

> Your ideas on resistance may have to do with the city you are living in, but there are many people living in Beirut that are producing very different kinds of work you are. How does your work deal with the conditions of the city?

Khoury: I would rather not talk about Beirut in general terms. I would much rather answer a question that is relative to a very specific building or situation. As a recent example, the design strategy of residential project Plot #1282 consisted of foreseeing the potentially catastrophic conditions that could arise in the near future due to the rapid development of the area in the absence of any master plan. All surrounding plots being private, the quasi-totality of the periphery of our plot could face blind walls defining the back of the future buildings around us. On this particular site, which has 406 meters of periphery, with only 5.5 meters intersecting public domains, the future does not look bright. Our building was shaped by a continuous setback along its periphery, and gradually offset inwardly on each floor. As the plan starts with a literal offset of the plot limit, it results in long, shallow, and elongated floor slabs. With facades open on all peripheral limits, we predict complete permeability, encouraging future developments to turn their faces to us rather than giving us their backs.

> How do you see your architecture in relation to other artist work that engages specific forms to produce meaning?

Khoury: The practice of architecture incorporates a number of other highly complex practices. It also involves dealing with financial realities. Designing and executing a building is a long process that can take many years. What

BERNARD KHOURY/DW5, YABANI (R2) JAPANESE
RESTAURANT, BEIRUT, LEBANON, 2002.

we produce, and the way we produce it, may seem very opaque for those who are not involved. I have the feeling that many artists and art critics are not only aware of the complexity of our practice, they are also impressed by the processes at work. This may sometimes lead to the overestimation of the intelligence of architects. I think that art practices are often more spontaneous than the practice of architecture. On that note, I do envy artists who most of the time get to choose their battlefields, go in and out of a situation more freely, and start and end a piece in very little time.

> Your "love of machines" is present in much of your work. How do you see the role of the mechanical in architecture?

Khoury: Machines of the mechanical age such as automobiles, trains, and planes have certainly celebrated modernity much more than architecture has. As we proceed into the electronic age, the fascination with the machine may seem outdated. However, it is important to note that architecture and the construction industry in general have not brought forward any major breakthroughs in the field of mechanical innovation. They have made reference to it, mimicked it, but not really produced any extraordinary inventions. On that note, I found Koolhaas's intervention at the 2014 Venice Architecture Biennale quite disappointing in the sense that it examined modern architecture through what seemed to me an etalage of very rudimentary mechanical equipment, which clearly shows how little architecture has invented on that level. I can understand the fascination with more complex and far more advanced mechanical inventions. For a long time, I was fascinated by the F-117 stealth bomber and many other military devices that pushed the limits of mechanical performance way beyond the field of construction. To compare architecture and other fields in terms of what the twentieth century has produced, and to be satisfied with what we've done would be quite sad.

> Circling back to this roughness as it relates to the world you practice in, a similar roughness can be seen in Arab world today. How should architecture respond to it?

Khoury: This roughness you refer to has to do with the difficult conditions of the territory. On that note, the conditions in Beirut are very different from those in what you refer to as the Arab world. One could say that Beirut is still a place where you can experience a sort of local modernity. Unfortunately, it is no longer the case as you go further east towards the new cities of the Gulf states, such as Doha or Kuwait City. At one point in time, Baghdad, Damascus, Cairo, as well as many other traditional Arab cities did aspire to be modern. This was the case not only for architecture, but also for other creative fields, such as cinema, music, theatre. These were the glorious years of the young Arab republics, before the notion of the nation-state went bankrupt. That signaled the end of the modern project on most of that territory. Modernity, in the contemporary Arab world, has become a commodity that can only be imported. This is very unfortunate.

Concerning Beirut, I would say that the difficult and sometimes sour realities an architect can confront could lead to the elaboration of very specific strategies and modes of survival. In my numerous attempts further east, I did believe every single time that what could be done in Riyadh, Kuwait, or any other Gulf city in fact, could not be possible anywhere else. But then again, all I see are blind imports, under-developed products of familiar models we have seen time and time again, from Shanghai to Dubai to Houston. This, in my opinion, is a sign of a cultural and political bankruptcy. I would have liked to see Arab cities turn their backs on the outdated global certainties, and invest more effort on understanding the very specific conditions which define their environments.

> If you would set the agenda for a new idea for the Arab world, what would that be?

Khoury: While the imported notion of the nation state has gone bankrupt in our part of the world, other forms of power and ideologies have emerged, and not for the better. At this point in time, the most effective acts of resistance are not taking place in the conventional territories of politics. In Lebanon for example, those have been hijacked by an incompetent and corrupt political class. Instead, I believe that there are other ways of acting on the political front, by producing meaning on territories that cannot be reached by the conventional political machines.

In the more stable territories of the western world, politics are practiced on conventional grounds. In our unstable world, we need to reinvent the political territories so we can produce meaning in the most improbable conditions. We have to think specifically, not generally. We have to start by recognizing the sometimes harsh realities of our contexts. We have to stop hiding all problematic questions under the carpet.

> The political situation creating this sterile imperfection, only pertains to the Arab world, or is a situation which applies to the whole world?

Khoury: The fact that our western cities have become dormant in their comfort is not such a good thing because it has annihilated the immunity of cities. Today, if I cut the electrical current here, for fifteen minutes, it would be a catastrophe! It would make the headlines tomorrow. This is just the beginning, so imagine some-body blowing himself up at the train station tomorrow, for some sort of cause you and I don't understand. We, on the other hand, have grown immune to these occur-rences. If anything, I am starting to feel safer in Beirut than I do in Paris.

> The modern movement started at a particu-lar moment. Does the crisis in the Arab world now produce a similar momentum that could result in a new beginning? Could it be a new beginning also for us, in the west?

Khoury: Who I am to answer your question? I don't know. I am not a futurist. The question is, do architects have a role in this? The rise and fall of modernism in the Arab world can be very clearly observed. But I do not see any clear project coming out of the current crisis in the Arab world. This looks more to me like the end of the idea of the greater Arab nation, and the great many illusions some of us had decades ago. I would not go as far as comparing it to the flimsiness of the European project, and the rise of nationalist tendencies in the old continent.

> Do you see your Johnnie Walker's "Keep Leb-anon Walking" campaign that features you as someone who managed to produce meaning in Beirut?

Khoury: I was on the 8:00 news, prime time, for thirty seconds every single day for a full year. I stood proudly on a 40 meter high billboard, way above a much smaller billboard that featured Paris Hilton. It was placed on one of the busiest arteries of Beirut. Architects do not typically get that kind of vulgar visibility. My intellectual friends did not endorse my crude and tasteless posture. To me, the experiment was worthwhile, as it was about transcending the conventional limits of communication with the public that are standard to architecture.

P. 7

KAZUYO SEJIMA (1956) is an architect. She studied architecture at the Japan Women's University, and established Kazuyo Sejima & Associates in 1987, after having worked with Toyo Ito. In 1995 she and Ryue Nishizawa co-founded the Tokyo-based firm SANAA (Sejima and Nishizawa and Associates). In 2010 she was the director of the Venice Architecture Biennale, the same year that she became the second woman to be awarded the Pritzker Architecture Prize, which she won, jointly, with Nishizawa for their SANAA work. Recent projects by SANAA include the Toledo Museum of Art Glass Pavilion in Toledo, Ohio (2006), the New Museum of Contemporary Art, in New York City (2007), and the Rolex Learning Center in Lausanne, Switzerland (2010). The College of Architecture (CoA) at the Illinois Institute of Technology (IIT) awarded their Grace Farms River Building, in New Canaan, Connecticut (2015), with the 2014–2015 Mies Crown Hall Americas Prize (MCHAP). Sejima has taught at Princeton University and Tama Art University, among other institutions.

P. 17

WILLIAM F. BAKER (1953) is a structural and civil engineer. He joined SOM in 1981, and has led its structural engineering practice for over twenty years. Baker is best known for the development of the "buttressed core" structural system, used in buildings such as the Burj Khalifa in Dubai. While regarded for his collaborative work on super-tall buildings, Baker's expertise also extends to long-span roof structures and specialty structures. Baker is a frequent collaborator with many artists, including James Carpenter ("Raspberry Island–Schubert Club Band Shell"), Iñigo Manglano-Ovalle ("Gravity is a Force to be Reckoned With"), James Turrell ("Roden Crater"), and Jaume Plensa ("World Voices"). He is a Fellow of both the ASCE and the IStructE, a member of the National Academy of Engineering, and an International Fellow of the Royal Academy of Engineering. Baker is an Honorary Professor at the University of Cambridge and has received honorary doctorates from the University of Stuttgart, Heriot-Watt University, and the Illinois Institute of Technology.

P. 33

WIEL ARETS (1955) is an architect. He received his MS in Architecture from the Eindhoven University of Technology, in 1983, where he co-founded *Wiederhall* and established WAA that same year, which now is based in Amsterdam, Maastricht, and Zürich. He has taught at AA London, Columbia, Cooper Union, and UdK Berlin, among others. From 1995 to 2001 he was Dean of the Berlage Institute, where he co-founded *Hunch*, and in 2012 he was appointed Dean of IIT CoA. In 2014 he established, at the CoA, the Mies Crown Hall Americas Prize (MCHAP). Projects by WAA include the Academy of Arts in Maastricht (1993), AZL Pension Fund in Heerlen (1995), Museum Hedge House in Wijlre (2001), Utrecht University Library in Utrecht (2004), Campus Hoogvliet in Rotterdam (2014), Allianz Headquarters in Zürich (2014), Schwäbisch Media in Ravensburg (2013), Jellyfish House in Marbella (2014), B' Tower in Rotterdam (2013), Anne van Bueren Tower in The Hague (2013), A' House in Tokyo (2014), IJhal Central Station in Amsterdam (2016) and The Double in Amsterdam (2017).

P. 51

JUNYA ISHIGAMI (1974) is an architect. Ishigami received his MA in Architecture and Planning from the Tokyo University of Arts in 2000. He worked with Kazuyo Sejima and Ryue Nishizawa at SANAA from 2000–2004, and in 2004, established junya.ishigami + associates. Projects have included the reconstruction of the Russian Polytechnic Museum in Moscow, the Kait Workshop at the Kanagawa Institute of Technology the Yohji Yamamoto store in New York City, and a winning design, in collaboration with Svendborg Architects, for The House of Peace (HOPE), a monument to peace in the harbor of Copenhagen. Since 2010 Ishigami has served as a professor at Tohoku University in Japan. In 2014 he was the Kenzo Tange Design Critic at the Harvard Graduate School of Design, and in 2015, he was named a visiting professor at the Princeton University School of Architecture. Ishigami received the Architectural Institute of Japan Prize in 2009, and was awarded the Golden Lion for Best Project at the 2010 Venice Architecture Biennale.

P. 61

STEFANO BOERI (1956) is an architect, writer and editor. In 1989 he received his PhD from the Istituto Universitario di Architettura di Venezia (IUAV), in Venice. He co-founded Boeri Studio (together with Gianandrea Barreca, Giovanni La Varra, 1998–2008), and then, Stefano Boeri Architetti (since 2008). Since 2014, he has led an office in Shanghai, in a partnership with Yibo Xu. Boeri has carried out a series of transformative projects for the re-use of urban waterfronts in places such as La Maddalena Marseille, Doha, Genoa, Naples, Trieste, and Thessaloniki. Boeri is a professor of Urban Planning at the Politecnico in Milan, and has been a guest professor at the Harvard Graduate School of Design, the Strelka Institute in Moscow, the Berlage Institute, and the Ecole Politecnique Federale de Lausanne. He is the director of a post-doctoral program at the Tongji University in Shanghai, where he leads Future City Lab (FCL), a multidisciplinary lab that explores urban biodiversity and forestation as a way to address climate change.

P. 77

PETER EISENMAN (1932) is an architect and educator. He holds MA and PhD degrees from Cambridge University, and honorary Doctorates of Fine Arts from the University of Illinois, Chicago, the Pratt Institute in New York City, and Syracuse University. In 2003, he was awarded an honorary Doctorate in Architecture by the Università La Sapienza in Rome. Eisenman founded in 1967 the Institute for Architecture and Urban Studies (IAUS), an international think tank for architecture in New York City, and was its director until 1982. His practice, Eisenman Architects, has designed private houses, educational institutions, and large-scale housing and urban design projects. He has taught at Cambridge University, Harvard University, Princeton University, Ohio State University, and The Cooper Union, and is currently the Charles Gwathmey Professor in Practice, at Yale. His many books include *Eisenman: Inside Out, Selected Writings 1963–1988* (2004); *The Formal Basis of Modern Architecture* (2006); and *Written into the Void: Selected Writings 1990–2004* (2007).

P. 93

RAFAEL VIÑOLY (1944) is an architect. He received his Diploma in Architecture from the University of Buenos Aires in 1968, and an MArch from the same university, in 1969. Viñoly opened his eponymous studio in New York City in 1983; the firm maintains offices worldwide in New York City and London, as well as satellite offices in Abu Dhabi, Buenos Aires, Chicago, and elsewhere. In 1989, he won an international competition to design the Tokyo International Forum, the largest and most important cultural complex in Japan. Other renowned work includes The Kimmel Center for the Performing Arts in Philadelphia, Pennsylvania; Jazz at Lincoln Center in New York City; the David L. Lawrence Convention Center in Pittsburgh, Pennsylvania; 20 Fenchurch Street in London; and 432 Park Avenue in New York City, the world's tallest residential tower. Viñoly is an International Fellow of The Royal Institute of British Architects. He has taught and lectured at cultural and educational institutions all over the world.

P. 107

BEN VAN BERKEL (1957) is an architect. He studied architecture at the Rietveld Academy in Amsterdam, and in 1987, received the AA Diploma with Honors from the Architectural Association of London. Together with his wife, Caroline Bos, he is the co-founder of UNStudio (United Network Studio). UNStudio has offices located in Amsterdam, Shanghai, and Hong Kong. Projects of the firm include the Mercedes-Benz Musuem in Stuttgart, Germany, the academic campus for the Signapore University of Technology & Design, the masterplan program for Arnhem Central in Arnhem, Netherlands, and the Dance Palace in St. Petersburg, Russia. The firm has been recognized with honors and awards from groups such as the London Design Awards, IF Design Awards, and the Council on Tall Buildings and Urban Habitat (CTBUH). Major publications on UNStudio and its work include *Delinquent Visionaries* (1993), *Mobile Forces* (1994), *Move* (1999), *UNStudio, Design Models* (2006), *Buy Me a Mercedes-Benz* (2006), *Reflections–Small Stuff by UNStudio* (2010), and *Knowledge Matters* (2016).

P. 125

PEZO VON ELLRICHSHAUSEN is the art and architecture firm of Mauricio Pezo (1973) and Sofia von Ellrichshausen (1976), which they co-founded in 2002. Pezo received an MArch at the Universidad Catholica de Chile in Santiago, in 1998; Von Ellrichshausen received her degree in Architecture from the Universidad de Buenos Aires, in 2002. Both teach at the Pontificia Universidad Católica de Chile in Santiago, Chile, and at the College of Architecture (CoA) at the Illinois Institute of Technology (IIT). They curated the Chilean Pavilion at the 2008 Venice Architecture Biennale, designed and built the Vara Pavilion at the 2016 Venice Architecture Biennale, and exhibited at the inaugural Chicago Architecture Biennial in 2015. Their work has been awarded with the MCHAP.emerge prize, the Rice Design Alliance Prize, the Iberoamerican Architecture Biennial Award, and the Chilean Architecture Biennale Award. They have been published in monographic issues of *A+U*, *2G*, and *Arq*, and their work is also part of the permanent collection of the MoMA, in New York City.

P. 139

PHYLLIS LAMBERT (1927) is an architect, photographer, lecturer, historian, and architecture and urbanism critic. Lambert received her MS in Architecture from the College of Architecture (CoA) at the Illinois Institute of Technology (IIT) in 1963. She is the Founding Director Emeritus of the Canadian Centre for Architecture (CCA) in Montréal, an international research center and museum founded in 1979, and is recognized internationally for her contributions to the advancement of contemporary architecture, for her concern for the social issues of urban conservation, and for the role of architecture in the public realm. Lambert first made architectural history as the Director of Planning of the Seagram Building in New York City (1954–1958), the development of which is documented in her book, *Building Seagram* (2013). She designed the Saidye Bronfman Centre for the Arts (1967), and prior to the establishment of the CCA, she founded Heritage Montreal, an organization dedicated to the preserving the architectural, historical, natural and cultural heritage of the greater Montréal region.

P. 163

RIKEN YAMAMOTO (1945) is an architect. He received his BA in Architecture from the Department of Architecture, College of Science and Technology at Nihon University in 1968. He was awarded an MA from Tokyo University of the Arts, Faculty of Architecture in 1971. In 1973 he founded the firm, Riken Yamamoto & Field Shop. Some of his recent works include Pangyo Housing in Seongnam, South Korea (2010). the Tianjin Library in Tianjin, China (2012) and winning design for the under-construction The Circle complex at Zurich Airport. He has received numerous awards, including the Japan Institute of Architects Award for the Yokosuka Museum of Art (2010), the Japan Arts Academy Award for Saitama Prefectural University (1999) and the Architectural Institute of Japan Prize for Future University of Hakodate (2000). From 2002 to 2007, he taught in the Department of Architecture at Kogakuin University. From 2007 to 2011 he taught at Yokohama Graduate School of Architecture at Yokohama National University. In 2011 he was named a visiting professor at Yokohama National University.

P. 197

HERMAN HERTZBERGER (1932) is an architect and theoretician. Hertzberger received his degree in Architecture and Engineering from the Delft University of Technology, in 1958, where he studied under Aldo van Eyck. That same year he opened his studio, HHA. Between 1959–1963 he was an editor of *Forum* magazine–an important structuralist magazine. The first project he won was a competition to design a student residence in Amsterdam. Hertzberger would go on to build many school buildings in the Netherlands during his career, including the Montessori School in Delft (1966), the Apollo (1983) and De Evenaar (1986) schools in Amsterdam, Polygoon in Almere (1992), and the Anne Frank School in Papendrecht (1994). His best-known work includes the Central Beheer in Appeldorn (1972), The Spui Theater Center, The Hague (1993), and The Chassé Theatre in Breda (1995). Hertzberger has taught at the Universities of Amsterdam, Delft, and Geneva, and was the founder and initial Dean of the Berlage Institute.

P. 195

ERWIN OLAF (1959) is a photographer. After initially studying journalism, he then turned to photography while exploring 1980s Amsterdam nightlife, from which he drew much of his early inspiration. In 1988, he established his reputation with the series, Chessmen, which was awarded the first prize in the Young European Photographer competition. His professional body of work has since grown to include commercial and fashion work, alongside personal and film projects. His films have been screened at leading museums and film festivals around the world, including the Centre Pompidou in Paris and the Museum at the Fashion Institute of Technology in New York City. He has taken part in numerous group and solo exhibitions internationally, including at the Maison Européenne de la Photographie, Paris; Museum voor Moderne Kunst Arnhem, Arnhem, Netherlands; Stedelijk Museum, Amsterdam; Bilbao Art Centre, Bilbao, Spain; and the Museum of the City of New York City, New York. His clients have included *Vogue*, Bottega Veneta, Diesel, and *The New York Times*.

P. 213

DAVID ADJAYE, OBE, (1966) is an architect. Adjaye received a BA from London South Bank University, and an MA in 1993, from the Royal College of Art in London. He established his studio, Adjaye Associates in London, in the 1990s, now with offices in London, New York City, and maintains a worldwide portfolio of projects. In the United States, Adjaye has recently completed a social housing scheme in New York City's Sugar Hill (2014) and the Ethelbert Cooper Gallery of African & African American Art at Harvard's Hutchins Center (2014). In 2016, his National Museum of African American History and Culture opened in Washington D.C. In 2015, a retrospective exhibition of his work was held at Haus der Kunst in Munich, and later at the Art Institute, in Chicago. Adjaye has taught at the Royal College of Art, the Architectural Association School, and has been a visiting professor at the University of Pennsylvania, Yale, Princeton and the Harvard Graduate School of Design.

P. 229

ARMAND MEVIS (1963) is a graphic designer. Mevis, together with Linda van Deursen, are co-founders of the internationally renowned graphic design studio, Mevis & Van Deursen. They both graduated from the Gerrit Rietveld Academy in Amsterdam in 1986, where they both received a BDes in Graphic Design. Mevis & Van Deursen mainly work for cultural clients, including the Stedelijk Museum in Amsterdam and the Museum of Contemporary Art Chicago. The firm has designed numerous books on architecture and design, as well as for publishing houses such as Walther König Verlag, JRP Ringier, and Hatje Cantz. The firm won the competition for the graphic identity for the City of Rotterdam as a designated Cultural Capital of Europe. Mevis is a design critic at the Werkplaats Typografie, Arnhem, the Netherlands and is a critic, as is van Deursen, at Yale University School of Art. Their work has been documented in the book, *Recollected Work: Mevis & Van Deursen*, published by Artimo, in 2005.

P. 243

DOMINIQUE PERRAULT (1953) is an architect. He received a Diploma in Architecture from the Ecole des Beaux-Arts in Paris, in 1978. He received a further degree in Urbanism from the Ecole Nationale des Ponts et Chaussees in 1979, and an MA in History from the École des Hautes Études en Sciences Sociales in Paris in 1980. He then established Dominique Perrault Architecture, in 1981. Perrault gained international recognition after winning the competition for the National French Library in Paris, in 1989. This project marked the starting point of many other public and private commissions abroad, such as the Velodrome and Olympic Pool in Berlin (1992), the European Court of Justice in Luxembourg (1996), the Olympic Tennis Center in Madrid (2002), the DC Tower in Vienna (2014), and the Poste du Louvre in Paris (2018). Since 2013, Perrault has been a Professor at the Ecole Polytechnique Fédérale de Lausanne, Switzerland, and serves as the director of the research laboratory for Underground Architecture (SUB).

P. 259

STAN ALLEN (1956) is an architect and educator. He received a BA from Brown University, a BArch from Cooper Union and an MArch from Princeton University. After working for Richard Meier in New York City and Rafael Moneo in Madrid, he established his independent practice in 1990. From 1999–2003, he worked in collaboration with James Corner/Field Operations. In 2007, SAA/Stan Allen Architect won an international competition for the redesign of Taichung Municipal Airport in Taiwan. Recently completed buildings include the Sagaponac House and the CCV Chapel in the Philippines. The firm has been recognized with P/A Awards for the Taichung Airport and the Yan Ping Waterfront in Taipei, AIA Awards for the CCV Chapel and Salim Publishing, among numerous other honors. Allen is the George Dutton '27 Professor of Architecture at Princeton University, and was the Dean of the Princeton University School of Architecture, from 2002–2012. In addition to teaching, he directs Princeton's Center for Urbanism, Architecture and Infrastructure.

P. 275

BERNARD KHOURY (1968) is an architect. He received his BFA and BArch from Rhode Island School of Design. He received an MArch from the Harvard Graduate School of Design, in 1993. After graduation, Khoury started an independent practice that, since, has developed a diverse portfolio of projects. In 2001, the municipality of Rome awarded him the honorable mention of the Borromini Prize, given to architects under the age of 40. Khoury is also the co-founder of the Arab Center for Architecture. He has lectured and exhibited his work in prestigious academic institutions in Europe and the United States, including a solo show of his work given by the International Forum for Contemporary Architecture at the Aedes Gallery in Berlin (2003), and numerous group shows, including SPACE at the opening show of the MAXXI museum in Rome (2010). He was the co-curator and architect of the Kingdom of Bahrain's national pavilion at the 2014 Venice Architecture Biennale.

This publication is an initiative of the Illinois Institute of Technology's College of Architecture, Chicago. The content was shaped by student interviews conducted as part of the "Dean's Lecture Series 2012–2017," introduced in NOWNESS 1.

Wiel Arets, the Illinois Institute of Technology, College of Architecture Dean and Rowe Family College of Architecture Dean Endowed Chair, would like to thank all those who made this publication possible: Illinois Institute of Technology, College of Architecture, the students whose curiosity drove the work, the faculty and staff, Vedran Mimica, Professor, Associate Dean of Research, Agata Siemionow, Visiting Assistant Professor, who has supported students through all interviews, the lecturers for their thoughtful engagement and responses, and all those who have generously supported the initiative.

Published by:
IITAC Press
IIT College of Architecture
3360 South State Street
Chicago, IL 60616-3793, USA
Phone +1 312 567 3230
www.arch.iit.edu

Actar Publishers
440 Park Avenue South, 17th Floor
New York, NY 10016
Phone +1 212 966 2207
salesnewyork@actar-d.com
eurosales@actar-d.com
www.actar.com

Editors: Wiel Arets, Agata Siemionow
Text Editing: John Bezold, Zehra Ahmed
Design: Edwin van Gelder, Mainstudio
Printing: Unicum, Tilburg,
the Netherlands
Binding: Boekbinderij van Mierlo,
Nijmegen, the Netherlands

Illinois Institute of Technology,
College of Architecture
Wiel Arets, Dean and Rowe Family
College of Architecture Dean
Endowed Chair
Ben Schulman, Director of Publishing
Travis Rothe, Senior Designer
Lluís Ortega, IITAC Editor
Vedran Mimica, Director of Research

The editors would like to thank James Carter, Jorge Serra De Freitas, Melanija Grozdanoska, Ko Simmel, Jenna Staff and Jing Jie Wong, for their assistance in the completion of this publication.

© of the edition, ITTAC and Actar
© of the texts, their authors
© of the images, their authors
All rights reserved
Printed in the Netherlands
ISBN: 9781945150500
Library of Congress Control Number: 2017941563
A CIP catalogue record for this book is available from Library of Congress, Washington, D.C., USA

The authors and Actar Publishers are especially grateful to the image providers. Every reasonable attempt has been made to identify owners of copyright. Should unintentional mistakes or omissions have occurred, we sincerely apologize. Such mistakes will be corrected upon notification in the next edition of this publication.

Participating
Students:
Jing Jie Wong
Melanija Grozdanoska
Jorge Serra de Freitas
Ko Simmel
Steven Karvelius
Reid Mauti
Trevor Simmel
Daniel Zweig
Phil Karczewski
Jenna Staff
Eleni Aroni
Sepideh Asadi
Skylar Moran
John Pasowicz
Keefer Dunn
Dan Costa de Baciu
Alfred To
Aaron Mikottis

Video recordings of the IIT Dean's Lecture Series, including the lectures of the interviewees featured in this book, can be viewed online at arch.iit.edu.

PHYLLIS LAMBERT, NOVEMBER 14, 2013

RIKEN YAMAMOTO, SEPTEMBER 2, 2015

HERMAN HERTZBERGER, MARCH 10, 2014

ERWIN OLAF, SEPTEMBER 21, 2016

DAVID ADJAYE, FEBRUARY 15, 2016

ARMAND MEVIS, FEBRUARY 17, 2016

DOMINIQUE PERRAULT, OCTOBER 8, 2013

STAN ALLEN, FEBRUARY 12, 2014

BERNARD KHOURY, APRIL 22, 2015